The principal objective of THE MATHESON TRUST is to promote the study of comparative religion from the point of view of the underlying harmony of the great religious and philosophical traditions of the world. This objective is being pursued through such means as audio-visual media, the support and sponsorship of lecture series and conferences, the creation of a website, collaboration with film production companies and publishing companies as well as the Trust's own series of publications.

The Matheson Monographs cover a wide range of themes within the field of comparative religion: scriptural exegesis in different religious traditions; the modalities of spiritual and contemplative life; in-depth mystical studies of particular religious traditions; broad comparative analyses taking in a series of religious forms; studies of traditional arts, crafts and cosmological science; and contemporary scholarly expositions of religious philosophy and metaphysics. The monographs also comprise translations of both classical and contemporary texts, as well as transcriptions of lectures by, and interviews with, spiritual and scholarly authorities from different religious and philosophical traditions.

IMAM 'ALI

FROM CONCISE HISTORY TO TIMELESS MYSTERY

'For whomever I am the *mawla*, 'Ali is his *mawla*.'

PROPHET MUHAMMAD

Imam ʿAli

From Concise History to Timeless Mystery

by

Reza Shah-Kazemi

TIIE MATHESON TRUST
For the Study of Comparative Religion

© Reza Shah-Kazemi, 2019

This first edition published by
The Matheson Trust
PO Box 336
56 Gloucester Road
London SW7 4UB, UK

www.themathesontrust.org

ISBN: 978 1 908092 18 2

British Library Cataloguing-in-Publication Data.
A catalogue record for this book is
available from the British Library.

Typeset by the publishers in Baskerville 10 Pro.

Calligraphies on cover and frontispiece
courtesy of Nuria García Masip
www.nuriaart.com
Cover design by Susana Marín.

Contents

Editor's Preface

In our times of frenzied news-seeking, it is easy to mistake the incessant flow of trivia for the originality of real art and craftsmanship, which makes the old new again every time. In fact, the word *news* has become meaningless, and finding new information, real *news*, becomes rarer with every passing day: not sneaky rehashes or bland summaries, but new knowledge, fresh from ever-flowing sources, elaborated in genuine ways with the selflessness and generosity of the authentic scholar who works *ad bonum commune*, for the benefit of everybody, sharing light. This is exactly what Reza Shah-Kazemi does with this book.

In his previous publications on Imam 'Ali, *Justice and Remembrance* (2007), and *Spiritual Quest* (2011), he had addressed contemplative aspects of the Imam's teachings in relation to mystical praxis, the principle of justice, and the hermeneutics of the Qur'an; this new work consolidates and approaches the subject from a more 'biographical' angle. The combined impression of these volumes is, for anyone interested in Islam, world religions or spirituality, that of an emerging iceberg, or rather more accurately, that of a long lost marvellous city which is discovered and brought to light, lovingly and painstakingly.

The life of 'Ali ibn Abi Talib, fourth caliph of early Islam and revered fountainhead of Shi'ite and Sufi lineages, 'is both inspirational and controversial: *intrinsically* inspirational and *extrinsically* controversial.' These words set the tone for what is a detailed and penetrating view of the figure of Imam 'Ali on various planes, the spiritual and ethical, the individual, the political and social. The author draws a unique kind of portrait in which the spiritual undercurrents of early Islamic history may be discerned at play, and where the sanctified heart of the Imam is revealed as a fulcrum of harmony between diverse and even divergent tendencies.

This book may be too Shi'a for some Sunnis, and too Sunni for some Shi'a, and it may be too political for some, and too spiritual for others, and so its main value lies precisely in a higher perspective where it reveals harmony, in a keen vision of the forces of *tawhid*, the drive to union, alive at the centre of historical events as in the hearts of men. It will have a cathartic effect upon the many, Sunnis and Shi'as alike, who wish to see 'Ali as a fountainhead of unity in Islam, not as a source of division. It makes accessible to both Muslims and non-Muslims the treasures of loving mercy flowing from 'Ali, a global paragon of initiatic wisdom.

In these days of urgent need for esoterism, of a return to the mettle of religion, where the intricacies and puzzling statements of theology are consumed in the fire of direct knowledge, the Matheson Trust is grateful and honoured to publish this contribution which is as timely and contemporary as it is traditional and timeless.

Juan Acevedo
Director
The Matheson Trust

A Note Concerning References

As the remit given to us was to make this short book as accessible as possible to a wide non-specialist readership, it was decided not to clutter the text with academic footnotes or endnotes. Instead, there will be a few references to some of the more important citations in parentheses in the text itself, with full details included in the Bibliography. References for almost all of the sayings of Imam 'Ali, and those of the Prophet, cited in this text can be found in two of our earlier works based on Imam 'Ali's teachings, *Justice and Remembrance: Introducing the Spirituality of Imam 'Ali*, and *Spiritual Quest: Reflections on Qur'anic Prayer according to the Teachings of Imam 'Ali*; and in the comprehensive 12-part article on Imam 'Ali in *Encyclopaedia Islamica*, published jointly by the Institute of Ismaili Studies and Brill. The few citations from Yasin al-Jibouri's translation of the *Nahj al-balagha* (the first complete, reliable translation directly from the Arabic) are indicated in parentheses in the text itself, as are several important sayings of Imam 'Ali translated by Tahera Qutbuddin in her excellent work, *A Treasury of Virtues: Sayings, Sermons and Teachings of 'Ali*, a translation of al-Qadi al-Quda'i's collection of sayings of Imam 'Ali, *Dustur ma'alim al-hikam*.

Introduction

The life of 'Ali ibn Abi Talib is both inspirational and controversial: *intrinsically* inspirational, one should say, and *extrinsically* controversial. We will focus on what is essential and inspirational in his life and thought, and ignore—as far as possible—the political, ideological and theological controversies that have, alas, obscured the radiance of his personality and the wisdom of his teachings. We do not aim to present here anything like a comprehensive biography, as this has been given in other works which can be easily consulted (see Bibliography). Rather, what we offer here is a series of reflections upon some of the essential elements of Imam 'Ali's life, basing these reflections on points of view opened up by his own teachings. These teachings are themselves applications of the principles conveyed by the essential sources of the Islamic revelation, that is, the Holy Qur'an and the spiritual reality of the Prophet, *al-Haqiqa al-Muhammadiyya*. These reflections on Imam 'Ali's life and teachings are intended to disclose the transformative nature of the ideals for which this great man lived and died—ideals which derive from the essence of the Islamic faith, but which also go to the heart of all authentic religions.

For the goal of Islam is nothing new; it aims to provide what every revealed religion provides: the means by which human beings can return to their original nature, created in the image of God. This original human nature is referred to in the Qur'an (30:30) as the *fitra*, and is defined in terms of 'the perpetually established religion' (*al-din al-qayyim*). This is religion as such, not such and such a religion. It is the spiritual quintessence of all religions, and thus reducible to none. It is the supra-temporal substance of religion, not one historical form of religion amongst others. Primordial human nature is at once universal and immutable: 'there is no changing the creation of God,' the Qur'an affirms, in relation to the *fitra* (30:30). It therefore informs and transcends all subsequent historical religions, for it is identical to integral, heartfelt faith: that knowledge and love of God which is woven into the human heart. According to Imam 'Ali, God's purpose in sending messengers to human beings is to remind them of the graces of God, and 'to unearth for them the hidden treasures of their intellects.' In other words, it is the purpose of all religious revelations to awaken, revive and actualise the knowledge and the love of God, these being the greatest spiritual 'treasures' of human consciousness, the celestial 'melodies' resounding in the depths of the heart of every human being.

The life of Imam 'Ali speaks with an eloquent tongue in a universal dialect to all those concerned with the possibilities of transcendence inherent in human consciousness. For his story heralds the triumph of the human spirit over the difficulties, tragedies and absurdities which are inevitable in what the Qur'an refers to repeatedly as 'the life of this lower world' (*al-hayat al-dunya*). Imam 'Ali had to overcome outward hardships and challenges throughout his life, and he also had to confront, as caliph, three brutal rebellions against his rule, in which, for the first time, Muslims were fighting fellow Muslims. So while the the first part of Imam 'Ali's life, in the blessed proximity of the Prophet, was glorious and heroic, the end of his life was grim and tragic, beset by confrontation and adversity, and cut short by the poisoned blade of an assassin. But this tragic ending pertains only to the outward story, for both his wisdom and his conduct, his words and his deeds, reveal a very different inner story.

That inner story presents us with extraordinarily compelling evidence of the way in which the Spirit (*al-Ruh*) can animate, guide and inspire the heart of a human being in all circumstances. The Spirit of God, breathed into man at his creation (15:29 *et passim*), is that which makes each and every human being inherently 'spiritual'. The human spirit, being in essence nothing other than the Spirit of God, can triumph over all manner of outer hardship, for it imparts the deepest peace, the greatest strength, and the clearest wisdom to which the human being has access. We may know this in principle, but Imam 'Ali helps us to see it in practice: indeed, to see it with dazzling self-evidence. And this is why contemplating the life of the Imam fortifies one's belief in the power, wisdom and goodness of the human spirit and, thereby, deepens one's faith in the source of that spirit, the Absolute.

His story shows us the kaleidoscopic range of virtues that flow from authentic faith. When, as we shall see in Chapter 2, he accepted the challenge to fight the pagan champion of the Quraysh, at the Battle of the Trench, the Prophet said: 'Faith (*iman*), in its entirety, confronts infidelity (*kufr*), in its entirety.' Similarly, the Prophet said to him: 'Only a believer will love you, O 'Ali, and only a hypocrite will hate you.' Such was the totality of Imam 'Ali's faith that it became something of a litmus-test or a touchstone. It brought to light the faith in the hearts of the faithful, this faith then being proved through their love for him; and at the same time it unmasked the hypocrisy of the hypocrites, their hypocrisy being betrayed by their hatred of him. The Prophet also referred to Imam 'Ali as the 'divider' or 'apportioner' (*qasim*) of Heaven and Hell, the meaning of which is connected to the principle that one's attitude to 'Ali reveals the measure of one's faith, and thereby, implicitly, one's fate in the Hereafter.

Imam 'Ali's absolute faith in God as the source of all power and knowledge, beauty and perfection, helps to account for the heights he attained in so many spheres of life and thought. He was a man of action and contemplation, being the greatest hero of his age as well as its wisest sage: as renowned for his chivalry as for his sanctity. In public, he delivered inspiring sermons from the pulpit, and in private he expounded the most esoteric teachings to his closest disciples. His teachings were delivered sometimes with Zen-like mystery, at other times with disarming simplicity; he eloquently expressed the most profound truths accessible to human intelligence, when this intelligence is suffused with perfect virtue. It is not surprising to find that so many of the founding figures of later intellectual disciplines in the Islamic tradition looked back to Imam 'Ali as the teacher who taught the teachers of their own teachers—claims that were to a very high degree substantiated by the historical record. The multi-faceted wisdom he imparted was therefore properly speaking 'seminal': it sowed the seeds for the formal articulation of such varied disciplines as Qur'anic exegesis, theology, philosophy, mysticism, jurisprudence, rhetoric (*balagha*) and grammar, calligraphy, together with various arcane sciences such as numerology (*jafr*) and alchemy. 'I am the city of knowledge,' said the Prophet, in one of his most famous indications of 'Ali's spiritual function, 'and 'Ali is its gate.' Imam 'Ali did indeed function, historically, as the 'gate' opening onto prophetic consciousness in the Islamic intellectual tradition. And he stands forth, after the Prophet himself, as the most stunning exemplar of what the mystical tradition of Islam refers to as 'the perfect human being', *al-insan al-kamil*.

◆

As is all too well known in our times, there are heated controversies between Sunnis and Shi'is over the status of 'Ali, centering on the question: was he, or was he not, designated by the Prophet as his successor? While our effort is to focus on the spiritual, intellectual and ethical principles opened up by 'Ali's life and thought, it is of course difficult to avoid altogether the issues attendant upon the Sunni-Shi'i divergence as regards his place in Islamic history and theology. Despite our effort to be as impartial as possible, this book will doubtless be seen as 'too Sunni' for some Shi'is, and 'too Shi'i' for some Sunnis. Be that as it may, the massive common ground between these two branches of Islam is where we take our stand. All Muslims agree on what is essential regarding 'Ali: that is, the essence of his personality and the wisdom of his teachings. This common ground has yielded particularly rich fruit in the fertile fields of Islamic spirituality—what is referred to chiefly as *tasawwuf*, or 'Sufism', in Sunni Islam; and *'irfan* ('spiritual knowledge') in the Shi'i world—despite the fact that there is significant overlap between the two traditions, and their roots are, practically speaking, identical.

Our perspective on 'Ali is derived from these spiritual and mystical traditions of Islam wherein he played a crucial, indeed, definitive role, second only to that of the Prophet himself. For 'Ali's name appears at the head of all the chains of transmission of the Sufi orders, the *silsila*s, that connect each master with his predecessor in the order. 'Ali serves as the crucial link between all these 'chains' of masters and the Prophet. These Sufi orders permeated the entire Muslim world, infusing the spirit of the Islamic revelation into the very flesh and blood of Muslim societies, Sunni and Shi'i, from Morocco in the west to the Malay archipelago in the east, from the Urals in northern Europe to the sub-Saharan regions of southern Africa. It is difficult to exaggerate the influence of Sufism in the matrix of Islamic civilisation, and particularly in relation to the legal and theological traditions of Islam, which Sufism aerated and balanced with its emphasis on spiritual values. Suffice to quote this revealing comment by one of the foremost historians of 'Islamicate' civilisation, Marshall Hodgson, in his still unsurpassed multi-volume history, *The Venture of Islam* (2:125):

> Sufism... became the framework within which all popular piety flowed together; its saints, dead and living, became

the guarantors of the gentle and co-operative sides of social life. Guilds commonly came to have Sufi affiliations. Men's clubs claimed the patronage of Sufi saints. And the tombs of local saints became shrines which almost all factions united in revering. It is probable that without the subtle leaven of the Sufi orders, giving to Islam an inward personal thrust and to the Muslim community a sense of participation in a common spiritual venture quite apart from anyone's outward power, the mechanical arrangements of the Shari'ah would not have maintained the loyalty essential to their effectiveness.

Wherever Sufism is present, the presence of Imam 'Ali will be felt. It was certainly no exaggeration when al-Junayd (d. 910), himself regarded as the 'master of the group' (*shaykh al-ta'ifa*) of the Sufis, claimed that 'Ali is 'our master as regards founding principles (*usul*),' and also as regards overcoming all 'trials and tribulations' (*bala'*) of this world.

What we aim to do, within the limits of this modest book, is to give the reader a taste of some of the ways in which Imam 'Ali's life and thought reveal these 'founding principles' of spirituality; and how he can teach us to overcome whatever trials and tribulations this world may throw at us. Our efforts have been guided by the writings of two Sufi masters in particular: Ibn 'Arabi (d. 1240), known as 'al-Shaykh al-Akbar' ('the greatest master'); and Jalal al-Din Rumi (d. 1273), known simply as 'Mawlana' ('our master'), or 'Mevlana' in Turkish—an epithet which is significant in relation to Imam 'Ali, who was designated by the Prophet as the *mawla* of all believing men and women. Both Ibn 'Arabi and Mawlana were profoundly attuned to the universal scope and mystical depth of Imam 'Ali's wisdom. In his magnum opus, *al-Futuhat al-Makkiyya*, Ibn 'Arabi writes that at the dawn of creation, when God manifested His light to the primordial 'dust' (*haba'*) in which the cosmos was contained in seed-form, 'that which possessed the greatest measure of receptivity to the light was the Reality of Muhammad... [and] the nearest of all human beings to the [Muḥammadan Reality] is ʿAli b. Abi Talib—may God be well pleased with him—imam of the world and the secret (*sirr*) of all the prophets' (Ibn ʿArabi, *Futuhat* [1269/1853 ed.] 1:132).

Similarly, Rumi refers to Imam ʿAli as 'the pride of every prophet and every saint' (*Mathnawi*, 1:3723). We shall turn repeatedly to Rumi's *Mathnawi*, and occasionally to poems in his *Diwan-i Shams* and passages in his *Discourses*, for help in understanding certain principles embodied, enacted, or elliptically stated by Imam ʿAli. The final narrative in volume 1 of the *Mathnawi* presents us with a magnificent portrait of Imam ʿAli, brimming with revealing insights, mystical implications and imaginative trajectories. In the course of this book, we shall refer to some of the precious ideas expressed in this inspired poetic portrait of Imam ʿAli.

◆

Unfortunately, the controversial issues surrounding Imam ʿAli are not only a question of history. They have indeed generated heated debate for over a millennium, but, in our times, they have resurfaced in a virulent and despicable manner. It is not a question here of blaming one side or the other; rather, it is incumbent upon all reasonable people to decry the fanatics and extremists of both sides, and to strengthen the bonds of understanding that exist between the overwhelming majority, that is, the (often too) silent, moderate majority within both Sunni and Shiʿi Islam. The disagreements between Shiʿis and Sunnis are insignificant in comparison with the common ground which they share. This commonality becomes clearer when seen in the light of the rich contribution that both schools have made to the exposition of the essential principles of the Islamic revelation, and to their crystallisation in the diverse arts, crafts, cultural and literary traditions of Muslim societies. Theological differences of opinion are marginalised both by the wisdom of the spiritual dimensions of Islam, and by the beauty of the 'civilisational' achievements of Muslim cultures worldwide.

In this context, it is important to stress that there is complete agreement between Sunnis and Shi'is as regards the three quintessential principles of Islamic faith, expressed as follows by one of the leading Shi'i theologians of our times, Ayatollah Ja'far Sobhani:

⋄ belief in the oneness of God (*tawhid*);

⋄ belief in the Qur'an as God's Revelation through Muhammad as His final Messenger (*risala*);

⋄ belief in the Resurrection of the soul, and Judgement in the Hereafter (*ma'ad*). (Sobhani, 144)

Just as there is a consensus among all schools of thought in Islam on these definitive tenets, there is, likewise, complete agreement about that which essentially defines 'Ali ibn Abi Talib: his sanctity (*walaya*), in comparison with which all theological, historical and political differences of opinion pale into insignificance. His sanctity eclipses all the other elements of his story. The sanctity he embodied is of a universal order, for it is compounded of spiritual principles which transcend time and space, religion and culture. So, when thinking of Imam 'Ali, we should always bear in mind the distinction between the particular and the universal, the timeless and the time-bound, the essential and the secondary, the principial and the phenomenal. This will help us to see the vast gulf, indeed, the incommensurability, between the contingent phenomena which make up the outward destiny of Imam 'Ali, on the one hand, and the transcendent principles that articulate his inner sanctity, on the other. It will also help us to appreciate the inspiring way in which the light of his sanctity triumphed over the shadows of this lower world; and it can help us to translate his triumph 'in the past' into practical lessons in the present, lessons which teach us how to address our own personal challenges, surmount our own particular difficulties, and make progress in our own quest to be faithful to our true nature, our *fitra*, 'according to which God created all human beings' (Q 30:30).

1

The Light of Sanctity
and the Veil of History

The aim of this book is to disclose some of the essential features of Imam 'Ali's sanctity, at the same time as presenting a brief account of the most significant events that are recorded in the outer chronicles of his life. We will try to interlace this short history with intimations of the Imam's inner mystery. What we mean by his 'mystery' is, basically, his sanctity, a quality which is unknowable in its essence, being rooted in the mystery of divinity itself, source of all sanctification and holiness; but which can be evoked or 'tasted' through its manifestations, and, in the case of the Imam, through his actions, teachings and his personality. In other words, we wish to encourage the reader to probe the mystery behind Imam 'Ali's persona, understanding the sanctity at the core of his persona as being both revealed and, paradoxically, concealed by the phenomena constituting his outward life. According to one etymology given for its Latin root, the word *persona* means 'mask'. The idea here is derived from actors on stage in Roman times: one has to discern the nature of the actor from the sound (*sonus*), the voice, that comes through (*per*) the mask. So *persona* has come to mean the role played by an actor in a play. Similarly, in respect of Imam 'Ali, the portrait of the person painted by the historical record is but a mask, a veil, through which we must make an effort to discern the sanctifying light (*nur al-walaya*) of this extraordinary being.

We will try to see his time-bound story in the light of his timeless wisdom, rather than allowing our view of this spiritual wisdom to be distorted by the contingent phenomena of mundane history. If we do this, we shall have a better chance of glimpsing the light of his sanctity through the veil of history. There is, however, an organic unity between his inner life and his outer comportment, between his spiritual wisdom and the enactment of this wisdom in his life in the world. The mysteries and trajectories opened up by Imam 'Ali's teachings are thus, as it were, embedded or encoded within his history; when we approach his life in this manner, history can help to reveal rather than conceal the metaphysical core of his teachings. The 'voice' of timeless wisdom and profound mystery might then be heard, coming through the 'mask' of chronological time and contingent history.

Mawla 'Ali

As we shall see in the following chapter, the Prophet famously declared at a pool called Ghadir Khumm: 'For whomever I am the *mawla*, 'Ali is his *mawla*.' The word *mawla* can be translated, in this context, as 'master' or 'patron'. As the Qur'an says: 'Know that God is your *mawla*: the most excellent *mawla*!...' (8:40). Linking this verse to the Ghadir declaration, we might say that God is declaring that whoever considers Him their *mawla* must consider *both* the Prophet and 'Ali as their *mawla*. This hierarchy of spiritual 'patronage' is based on the principle of *walaya*, a principle that is both unique and unifying. The two words *mawla* and *wali* share the same root, and are in fact synonyms; they both mean 'possessor of *walaya*' (in addition to several other meanings). It is important here to address the meaning of *walaya*, as this is axiomatic

2

for our understanding of the sanctity of Imam 'Ali, the most important key for unlocking the spiritual treasure of his mystery. It cannot be translated by a single word in English, as it connotes the following meanings: sanctity, guardianship, patronage, authority, proximity, initiatic power, friendship, loving devotion, orientation, affiliation. One who has this quality is called a *wali*, the plural of which is *awliya'*: these 'friends of God' are what would be called 'saints' in English, although the two notions only partly overlap, there being significant differences between the Islamic conception of *walaya* and the Christian idea of sainthood (see for discussion, Chodkiewicz, *Seal, passim*). In Muslim belief, all the prophets are saints, but not all saints are prophets. It should be noted that the angels also refer to themselves as *awliya'*, which, in this context, means 'guiding friends':

> Those who say: 'Our Lord is God,' and are upright thereafter, the angels descend upon them [saying]: 'Fear not, and grieve not; and hear the good news of the Garden which you are promised. We are your guiding friends, in the life of this world and in the Hereafter' (Q 41:30).

Just as angelic forces guide, demonic forces deceive and mislead: these forces being referred to as the *awliya'* of the devil (Q 4:76). God Himself is described as *al-Wali*, as we shall see in a moment. He is also described as *al-Mawla*, as just noted. In addition to calling 'Ali the *mawla* of the believers, the Prophet also referred to him as the *wali* of the believers. In one narration, as found in an important compilation of Ahmad al-Nasa'i—writer of one of the four canonical compilations of *hadith*s in Sunni Islam—entitled *Khasa'is Amir al-mu'minin* ('The Special Qualities of the Leader of the Faithful')—we read the following statement by the Prophet: "Ali is part of me and I am part of him, and he is the master (*mawla*) of every believer after me' (Nasa'i, *Khasa'is*, 62).

What needs to be stressed here is that the quality of

3

walaya is at once divine in essence and human (as well as angelic) as regards manifestation, the divine quality being expressed through human intermediaries, by refraction. This unitive principle is understood from what is arguably the single most important verse of the Qur'an alluding to Imam 'Ali's sanctity: 'Truly your *Wali* is only God, and His Messenger, and those who believe—those who observe prayer and pay the alms-tax while they bow down [in prayer]' (5:55). Many commentaries have been made on the meaning of this verse, but there is broad agreement among the exegetes, Sunni and Shi'a alike, that the occasion for its revelation was as follows. A beggar came into the mosque asking for alms; Imam 'Ali was performing the canonical prayer, but heard the beggar's request for help, and pointed to his ring, indicating that the beggar should take it and sell it. It is important to note he made this indication while in the bowing posture (*ruku'*) of the prayer (that is, the very posture referred to in 5:55, which is bowing down from the waist, as opposed to bowing down in prostration, one's head touching the earth, *sujud*). So 'Ali is being referred to, implicitly, through the plural form, 'the believers', the whole category of believers being as it were symbolised by this one 'believer'. As noted above, the Prophet referred to 'Ali as 'faith, in its entirety.'

The mystical import of this, and several other verses and prophetic statements, is that the quality of *walaya* pertains in the first instance to God, and then, by refraction, is manifested through the Prophet (and by implication all prophets) and through Imam 'Ali (and by implication all 'believers' who have attained the rank of sainthood, whatever their religion). This rank is described in the following *hadith qudsi*, a saying in which God speaks in the first person, through the Prophet; it is accepted as authentic by both Sunni and Shi'i scholars of *hadith* and is to be found in the canonical collections of both schools of thought:

My servant draws near to Me through nothing I love

more than that which I have made obligatory for him. My servant never ceases to draw near to Me through supererogatory acts until I love him. And when I love him, I become his hearing by which he hears, his sight by which he sees, his hand by which he seizes, and his foot by which he walks.

This saying is preceded by the words: 'whoever opposes a friend (*wali*) of Mine, I declare war on him.' Therefore the extraordinary modes of cognition and action ascribed to the one whom God 'loves' are so many ways of describing the divine dynamic operating through the entire being of the *wali Allah*, the 'friend of God', the saint. He sees God because it is in truth God who 'sees' through him, inasmuch as he, the saint, has seen 'through' the veil of his own selfhood, realising the deepest truth of the first testimony: *la ilaha illa'Llah*, 'no divinity (reality) but God (the sole Reality).' Thus, as it is said in the Sufi tradition, none comes to see 'Him to whom nothing is similar' but 'Him to whom nothing is similar'; in other words, none sees God but God. This fundamental principle of Islamic spirituality is articulated by Imam 'Ali in the following aphorism, as simple as it is profound: 'Know God through God' (*i'rafu'Llah bi'Llah*). The vision which the saint enjoys is a vision of God by God through God: that is, as regards the subject of vision, as regards the object seen, and as regards the medium—the light—through which the vision takes place.

The light in question radiates from the illumination of divine *walaya*, for indeed, it is the very function of *walaya* to illuminate and enlighten: 'God is the *Wali* of those who believe. He brings them forth from the darknesses into the Light' (Q 2:257). If God, as *al-Wali*, brings enlightenment to the believers, so too does the saint as *wali Allah*, or rather: God alone brings enlightenment, whether through direct Revelation, or mediated through His 'friends', the prophets and the saints, whose complete self-effacement before God renders them, in some indefinable but nonetheless palpable

5

way, transparent to the light of God, the only light there is: 'God is the light of the Heavens and the earth' (Q 24:35).

The Prophet makes a remarkable statement about Imam 'Ali—a *hadith* found in the collections of both Shi'i and Sunni Islam: 'Looking at the face of 'Ali is an act of worship' (*al-nazar ila wajhi 'Ali 'ibada*). The most obvious meaning of this (at first sight) baffling statement is that seeing a saint reminds one of God, and being reminded of God (or simply: remembering God) is an act of worship. One thinks here of the contemplative function of icons in Christian worship (see for discussion Williams, 2002), and of the role of *darshan*, the 'witnessing' of a holy person or divine image in Hinduism (see Eck, 2007). Indeed, according to the Qur'an, remembrance of God is the greatest act of worship: 'Establish the prayer (*al-salat*); truly the prayer keeps one away from shameful and wrong deeds. But the remembrance of God is greatest (*wa la-dhikru'Llahi akbar*)' (29:45). So, on the simplest level of contemplation, if looking at the face of this great saint induces a state of remembrance of God, it can be referred to as an act of worship. As the Prophet said, describing the 'friends of God', *awliya' Allah*: 'When they are seen, God is remembered.'

The repercussions of this act of worship will vary according to the depth of the comprehension, and the quality of the contemplation, of the person engaging in this implicit act of worship. Most importantly, perhaps, the devotee should be aware that 'Ali's spiritual station as the *wali Allah*, the saint or beloved 'friend' of God, is an embodiment or exteriorisation of the inner reality of the Prophet—the *Haqiqa Muhammadiyya*. According to the mystical tradition of Islam, *walaya* is the inner dimension of prophethood (*batin al-nubuwwa*). Understanding this inner relationship will help the devotee to see that the mystery in the affirmation, *'Aliyyun wali Allah*, "'Ali is the Friend of God,' leads to a more profound comprehension of the meaning of the second testimony of Islam: *Muhammadun rasul Allah*, 'Muhammad is the Messenger of God.' The inner

reality or mystery of the 'Messenger', is that he is a perfect revelation or manifestation of God. The divine Reality which is
absolutely unknowable in Its Essence makes Its Names and
Qualities knowable through the mirror of the Messenger. So,
the inaccessible transcendence of the Essence—expressed in
the formula *la ilaha illa'Llah*—is compensated by the manifestation of the Names and Qualities of the Essence reflected by the
Messenger, thereby making these divine Qualities both accessible to human beings and assimilable by them. The Prophet is
the embodiment both of *walaya*, the inner dimension of prophethood, and of prophethood itself, *nubuwwa*. Whereas Imam
'Ali is the embodiment of *walaya*, not of *nubuwwa*. He therefore makes more explicit that which is implicit or hidden in
the Prophet's prophethood: hence the many sayings of Imam
'Ali which relate to the esoteric dimension, the inner aspect of
the Prophet's message, and of the Prophet's nature, pertaining to the *haqiqa*, spiritual reality. In his allusions to his own
mystery, then, Imam 'Ali is unavoidably alluding, *a fortiori*, to
the mystery of the Prophet, to the *Haqiqa Muhammadiyya*, or
the *Nur Muhammadiyya*, 'the Muhammadan Light.'

Imam 'Ali thus helps us to understand how the mystery
of divinity, the ultimate *Haqiqa*, is at least partially opened
up by the mystery of the Prophet, the *Haqiqa Muhammadiyya*;
and how the mystery of *walaya*, accessible in principle to every
human being, evokes a synthesis of the mysteries of divinity,
prophethood, and humanity. All three mysteries pertain to
beauty, *husn*: the divine Nature is described in terms of the
'most beautiful Names' of God (*al-asma' al-husna*, see Q 17:110
et passim); the Prophet is not just an exemplar, but a 'beautiful'
role-model (*uswa hasana*, see Q 33:21); and every believer is
bound to follow the Prophet for the sake of that beauty of
soul, *ihsan* (literally, 'making beautiful') which enables the
soul to consummate its love of God, such love being the
very reason for following the Prophet: 'Say [O Prophet, to
the people]: If you love God, follow me; God will love you'

(Q 3:31). Hence the prophetic saying: 'Assume the character-traits of God (*takhallaqu bi-akhlaqi'Llah*),' alluding to these three degrees of spiritual beauty.

The Beauty of Truth

'Know the Truth, and then you will know its people (*ahl*),' the Imam tells us. Do not think you can come to the Truth, he adds, simply by knowing 'its people.' Again: 'look at what is said, not who has said it.' In relation to the phenomenon constituted by Imam 'Ali, then, if we wish to discern his true reality (*haqiqa*), we can only do so in the measure that we have assimilated the Truth as such, *al-Haqq*.

So our search for deeper significance in the life of Imam 'Ali cannot be divorced from our own personal quest for meaning; on the contrary, our own quest can help us to see him and ourselves in the light of the spiritual Truth, which Imam 'Ali never ceased to stress in his teachings. He wishes us to cultivate and deepen our own discernment, rather than simply engage in praise and imitation of those who are deemed to be enlightened, those who may be called 'the people of the Truth.' While it is no doubt true that, in our spiritual quest, our initial orientation towards the Truth requires teachers and guides, the point the Imam is making in these sayings is that we must make an active effort to realise, 'to make real' (through *tahqiq*) within our hearts the truths that our guides are teaching us. Such truths given to us from 'without' awaken us, making us aware that those truths and the realities to which they correspond, are already within our deepest consciousness. Then we will be able to see who the 'people of Truth' are: we will have discovered our own inner discernment, recognising in such souls as Imam 'Ali a perfect embodiment of the Truth which we have already recognised, to some degree, within ourselves. Our inner discernment will also reveal to us the incommensurable chasm separating our own 'embodiment' of the Truth from his: we will see our own imperfections more clearly in the mirror of his perfection.

The aim of divine revelation is to remind us of truths we have forgotten. According to Sermon 1 of the *Nahj al-balagha*:

> God sent to humanity His messengers, dispatching prophets in succession, in order to claim from His creatures the fulfilment of the covenant of His creation; to remind them of His forgotten graces; to remonstrate with them through communication [of His Revelation]; *to unearth for them the buried treasures of the intellects*; and to show them signs of omnipotence: the outspread earth laid low beneath them, provisions which give them life, finalities which mete out death; ailments hastening their decrepitude, and a succession of events that flow over them (emphasis added).

It is as if the Imam is saying: enlighten yourself by means of the twofold light God has already given you: the light revealed through scripture, and the light breathed by God into your own intellect, resulting in 'treasures' which are, for the majority, buried under the rubble of forgetfulness. The Truth given to us by God through prophetic revelation, and by our teachers through formal instruction, must resonate with, and thus awaken, the Truth that resides in the depths of our own heart. And it is only because they resonate with that inner Truth that the spiritual, intellectual and ethical precepts imparted from 'on high' stimulate the aspiration for an ever more profound conformity to the Truth, and an ever more transformative assimilation of the Truth.

This is one of the most important of all the intellectual principles taught to us by Imam 'Ali. It opens up to us the means by which we can attain the spiritual essence of the intellect, leading us away from a merely cerebral conception of things to a heartfelt realisation of the ultimate reality of things. This, in accordance with the well-known supplication of the Prophet: 'O Lord, show us the ultimate reality of things (*haqa'iq al-umur*),' and with the simpler expression of the same prayer for pure objectivity: 'Our Lord, show us things as they are' (*Rabbana arina'l-ashya' ka-ma hiya*). To the degree that we are shown things as they truly are, we shall, in that measure see that what the prophets and the saints manifest is our own deepest reality. Rumi teaches us this lesson in a most revealing manner, in a reflection on one of the deeper meanings of the verse 'Truly there has come unto you a Prophet from yourselves (*minkum*)' (Q 9:128):

> In the composition of man all modes of knowledge were originally commingled so that his spirit might show forth all hidden things, as limpid water shows forth all that is under it... and all that is above it, reflected in the substance of water. Such is its nature, without treatment or training. But when it was mingled with earth or other colours, that property and that knowledge was parted from it and forgotten by it. Then God Most High sent forth Prophets and Saints, like a great, limpid water such as delivers out of darkness and accidental colouration every mean and dark water that enters into it. Then it remembers; when the soul of man sees itself unsullied, it knows for sure that so it was in the beginning, pure, and it knows that those shadows and colours were mere accidents. Remembering its state before those accidents supervened, it says, *This is that sustenance which we were provided with before* (Q 2:25). The Prophets and the Saints therefore remind him of his former state; they do not implant anything new in his substance. Now, every dark water that recognises that great water, saying, 'I come from this and I belong to this,' mingles with that water... It was on this account that God declared: *Truly there hath come unto you a Prophet from yourselves* (9:128) (Rumi, *Discourses*, 44–45).

He reinforces the teaching in another discourse: 'Those who acknowledge the truth see themselves in the Prophet and hear their own voice proceeding from him and smell their own scent proceeding from him.' To deny the Prophet is tantamount to denying one's own reality. 'No man denies his own self. Therefore the Prophets say to the community, "We are you and you are we; there is no strangeness [i.e., alienation or otherness] between us"' (*Discourses*, 227).

♦

So, following the Prophet's example, Imam 'Ali's intention is to stimulate and awaken our intelligence, helping us to see the Truth for ourselves, using our own intellectual, spiritual, and ethical resources, and not simply blindly imitating (through *taqlid*) some putative authority. To use one's 'ethical' resources for the sake of deepening our intelligence sounds strange to the modern ear: what has ethics got to do with intelligence? It has everything to do with it, for in the Imam's perspective, the intelligence cannot realise its full, God-given potential in the absence of ethical purity; if there is no beauty of soul—that inner beauty which is woven out of all the essential virtues— there can be no depth of intelligence. If the soul is lacking in virtue, the intellect will be stunted, or disfigured.

'The excellence of the intellect,' Imam 'Ali tells us, 'resides in its capacity to perceive the beauty of outwardly manifest things (*zawahir*), and inwardly hidden ones (*bawatin*).' In other words, one must retrace the outward forms of beauty to their invisible archetypes, which are located both within the heart and in Paradise—both 'places' being symbols of degrees of consciousness, the one subjective and microcosmic, the other objective and macrocosmic. This can be seen as an elaboration upon the prophetic teaching: 'God is beautiful and He loves beauty.' The true intellectual sees the beauty of all things, formal and outward, essential and inward. The beauty thus perceived radiates through his intelligence into his character,

11

deepening and enriching all the fundamental virtues. The intellectual is therefore not someone who has accumulated a huge amount of data and has an impressive power of recall. Rather, the truly intelligent person is one in whose soul all the essential virtues are present—at least to some degree (through good intention and sincere effort), if not in all their plenitude; because the virtues contribute in a vital way to the process by which the spiritual essence of the intelligence is brought to fruition.

There are many sayings of the Imam in which the intellect is described as deficient if it lacks such and such a virtue— humility, sincerity, forbearance, courtesy, restraint, generosity, kindness, patience, contentment, gratitude, and so on. The intellect is also deficient if it lacks joy: the most joyous of people is the intellectual, Imam 'Ali tells us. The intellectual is also one from whom love radiates. 'Loving (*al-tawaddud*) is half of the intellect,' he says. Imam 'Ali cannot but manifest love, because he objectively perceives and subjectively assimilates beauty; and just as God 'loves beauty,' the Imam cannot help loving beauty, to which his love is drawn by spiritual magnetism. Without the radiance of love, and without beauty of soul, there can be no completeness or integrity of intelligence. By contrast, if the intelligence is activated and deepened by love and beauty, it will more acutely perceive the truth of the prophetic teaching that 'God is beautiful, and He loves beauty.' The intelligence will then be enriched by the harmonious interplay between knowledge, love and virtue, all three qualities opening the 'eye' of the heart, allowing it to see God: 'Eyes see Him not according to outward vision; rather, hearts see Him according to the realities of faith (*haqa'iq al-iman*),' the Imam tells us, in a statement which can be read as the positive counterpart to this verse of the Qur'an, describing the reason why it is that disbelievers do not believe in God: 'It is not the eyes that are blind; rather, blind are the hearts within their breasts' (22:46).

12

If, however, these virtues and qualities are lacking in the soul, then an intelligent person, objectively aware of his limitations, will engage in what the Prophet called the 'greatest struggle' (*al-jihad al-akbar*), the spiritual battle against the vices or faults of the soul. In the words of Imam 'Ali: 'Struggling against the soul through knowledge—such is the mark of the intellect.' In this connection Imam 'Ali teaches us something most inspiring about the principle of *rahma*, which we can translate not just as mercy and compassion but as *loving* mercy and compassion, the element of 'love' being essential to the meaning of the word, which is etymologically related to the word for 'womb' (*rahim*). A clear evocation of the maternal love that is inherent in this notion was given by the Prophet, when, during the peaceful conquest of Mecca, he compared the *rahma* of a mother for her new-born babe with the *rahma* of God towards all human beings—the latter of course being infinitely greater, but the point is that both maternal love and divine love are manifestations of the same essential quality, emanating from the divine and inspiring the human. According to a holy utterance, in which God speaks in the first person, 'I derived My Name, *al-Rahman*, from the word *rahim* (womb).'

Against this background, Imam 'Ali's description of the greatest spiritual struggle is most revealing: he tells us that it is *rahma* which will empower the intellect in its struggle against the soul's vices and faults. Within the soul, the intellect is the commander of the 'forces' of *al-Rahman*; while egoistic desire (*hawa*) is the commander of the 'forces' of *al-Shaytan* (the Devil). Through this image he teaches us that in this, the greatest of all struggles, we must always have a spiritual sense of the infinite power flowing from divine mercy. It is not our own efforts, however indispensable they be, that will enable us to triumph in the greatest struggle of all; it is the absolute power of God, manifesting as merciful love and compassion, which will give us victory: our efforts serve to attract this empowering grace, in the measure of our moral and spiritual conformity to the requirements of divine mercy. 'The dispensing of mercy brings down upon one [divine] mercy,' the Imam tells us; and again: 'I am astounded by the person who hopes for mercy from one above him, while he is not merciful to those beneath him.'

This emphasis on *rahma* helps us to understand what otherwise might be a paradox concerning the character of Imam 'Ali. For, on the one hand, he was renowned for his rigorous—some would say severe—sense of justice, together with all the virtues that one associates with a warrior of his formidable reputation, virtues such as courage, discipline, vigilance and so on. However, on the other hand, we are told in the sources that he had a 'gentle disposition' (*lin janib*), that he led with 'a light touch', that he was known for the 'charismatic ease of his character' (*sajahat al-akhlaq*) and for the 'joyfulness of his countenance' (*bishr al-wajh*). As we shall see in Chapter 3, these character traits of Imam 'Ali became proverbial, to the point that his enemies at the Battle of Siffin exploited his gentle qualities in their propaganda campaign against him: such a man, they said, was too light-hearted to be taken seriously as a leader. What his enemies apparently failed to realise was that Imam 'Ali's happy disposition was the outward expression of an other-worldly joy, which he was constantly experiencing in the depths of his heart, despite the terrible trials he was enduring. The Imam tells us that his heart is already in Paradise, only his body is 'at work' in this world. He is one who rejoices in his 'intimacy with the spirit of certainty (*ruh al-yaqin*), making easy what the extravagant find harsh, and befriending that by which the ignorant are alienated.' He is immersed in the depths of *spiritual* joy through his intimate contact with the *spirit* of certainty (*ruh al-yaqin*), because that of which he is certain is nothing other than God, and God is pure *rahma*: mercy and compassion, inseparable from love, beauty and beatitude. Intimate contact with the source of infinite beatitude imparts supernatural happiness; that is, it bestows such a profound degree of spiritual joy and inner peace upon the heart, upon the inmost core of consciousness, that no outward affliction from the world can unsettle it. Only the outer surface of the soul can be affected by outward tribulation, the heart remaining at peace. 'The believers are well in all circumstances,' the Prophet said. In other words, the *true* believer, one in whose heart faith has become deepened into certainty, is permanently in a state of divine remembrance, and thereby at peace: 'Those who believe and whose hearts are at peace in the remembrance of God: is it not in the remembrance of God that hearts are at peace?' (Q 13:28).

The Speaking Qur'an

'The Qur'an consists of a book inscribed, between two covers; it speaks not with a tongue, it cannot do without an interpreter' (*tarjuman*). Imam 'Ali was the interpreter of the Qur'an par excellence for his generation, following the death of the Prophet. He claimed that 'Not one verse has been revealed of which I know not where it was revealed, what it concerns and its subject matter.' According to several narrations, he knew the circumstances of the revelation (*asbab al-nuzul*) and the inner meaning of every verse; all abrogating and abrogated verses; those of definite (*muhkam*) and those of polyvalent (*mutashabih*) meaning (referring to 3:7); and those of general (*'amm*) or particular (*khass*) applicability. He taught, following and reinforcing the Prophet's teachings, that the Qur'an has a variety of aspects (*wujuh*), each verse having seven or seventy levels of meaning. He claimed be able to load seventy camels with the pages of a commentary he could give on the *Fatiha*, the opening chapter of the Qur'an, consisting of seven verses. This claim is not quite so fantastic as may appear at first sight, given the multiple levels of meaning in each verse of the

Qur'an, the polysemic nature of the Arabic language (and thus the semantic fields of significance opened up by virtually every single word of the revealed Speech), and in the light of the following hermeneutical principle of the Imam, which was to establish an entire genre of exegesis known as *tafsir al-Qur'an bi'l-Qur'an* ('the explanation of the Qur'an by the Qur'an'): 'The Book of God is that by means of which you see, speak and hear. Parts of it speak through other parts, and some parts of it bear witness to other parts.'

If therefore we wish to explore any idea expressed in any verse of the Qur'an, we need to study many other verses which contain meanings and implications which have a bearing on that idea. We need, on the one hand, to have a comprehensive knowledge of the Qur'an; and on the other hand we need to exercise our intuition in relation to the potentially unlimited allusions, hints, and intimations (*isharat*) that each verse, and each word of the revealed discourse contains. These allusions fly like sparks from the words and verses in one part of the Qur'an, casting light on nuances of meaning being expressed, explicitly or implicitly, in other parts of the Qur'an. We are thus plunged into an unfathomably profound and unimaginably intricate nexus of interwoven themes and reciprocally illuminating truths. We see how the Qur'an is indeed 'a clarification of *everything*' (16:89; emphasis added); how it contains the seeds of the solution to every conceivable question pertaining to metaphysics, cosmology, spirituality, psychology, ethics, law and society; how someone like Imam 'Ali could indeed write camel-loads of pages of commentary on just seven verses of the text. All that exists in the cosmos, and beyond it, is either expressed or intimated within a matrix of discourse, a revealed tapestry woven out of principles, images, allusions symbols, similitudes, and parables intertwining in infinitely varied patterns: 'And indeed, We have expounded in this Qur'an every kind of image-similitude (*mathal*) for mankind' (18:54).

Imam 'Ali was, however, much more than just a commentator and interpreter of the Qur'an: he referred to himself as 'the speaking Qur'an' (*al-Qur'an al-natiq*). He made this claim when his opponents at the Battle of Siffin (see Chapter 3) hoisted pages of the Qur'an on their spears, appealing to the Word of God for arbitration. He was not merely engaging in battlefield rhetoric. In another saying, he tells us: 'Everything in the Qur'an is in the *Fatiha*; everything in the *Fatiha* is in the *Basmala* [the formula of consecration, the first verse of the chapter: *Bismi'Llah al-Rahman al-Rahim*, 'In the name of God, the Compassionate, the Merciful']; everything in the *Basmala* is in the *ba'* [the letter 'b']; everything in the *ba'* is in the dot [beneath it]: and I am that dot.'

We may be able to understand better what the Imam means by this extraordinary claim, to be one with the quintessence of the entire Qur'an, if we take into account his application of the concept of *tajalli*, 'Self-disclosure', or theophany (the manifestation of God through phenomenal form and spiritual energy). This notion can be complementarily juxtaposed with *tanzil* (or *nuzul*), which is the 'descent' of the Qur'an, the revelation, or bringing into the world, of the divine discourse. To refer to the Qur'an as a *tajalli* means that it is not simply the revelation of the message of God; rather, it means that the Qur'an is, in and of itself, a theophanic Self-disclosure, a manifestation of something of the very Being of God, of the Divine 'substance' or 'energy', mediated by melodic sound and meaningful speech. The Imam says: 'He has theophanised Himself to them [His creatures] in His Book' (*fa-tajjala lahum fi kitabihi*). He also describes God as one who has theophanised Himself (*mutajalli*), to His creatures *by means of* His creatures (*li-khalqihi bi-khalqihi*). The whole cosmos, in other words, manifests the divine to the creatures, in a way analogous to the manifestation of God to His creatures through the Qur'an: both the cosmos and the Qur'an are modes of theophany. The Qur'an can thus be concretely

17

perceived—and not just abstractly conceived—as a sonoral and textual recapitulation of the entire cosmos; while, for its part, the cosmos can be seen as the Qur'an writ large.

Just as Imam 'Ali indicated the correspondence between the Qur'an and the whole of creation, so the Prophet alluded to an equally mysterious correspondence, between the Qur'an and the Imam: 'The Qur'an is incumbent upon you, so take it as an *imam* and a leader (*qa'ida*).' This *hadith* can be read most profitably in the light of another, more famous one, in which the Prophet refers to his legacy: 'Truly, I am leaving behind amongst you the two weighty things (*al-thaqalayn*): the Book of God and my Ahl al-Bayt, they will not be parted from each other until they return to me at *al-hawd* [the paradisal pool].' Similarly, we have this saying of the Prophet: ''Ali is with the Qur'an and the Qur'an is with 'Ali. They will not separate from each other until they return to me at *al-hawd*.' The spiritual substance of 'Ali is at one with that of the Qur'an, such that he could without exaggeration call himself a 'speaking Qur'an.' However, according to Imam 'Ali, each human being can be regarded, in one sense, as a divinely revealed 'book'; for the human being, made in the image of God, is properly speaking a theophany. As we have already seen, God makes Himself manifest, as *al-mutajalli*, to His creatures by means of His creatures; so each human being is a microcosm, a 'small world', by means of which God reveals Himself. This idea is marvellously expressed in one of Imam 'Ali's most famous couplets:

> Although you see yourself as an insignificant speck,
> within you the entire universe is encapsulated;
> You are thus yourself the *meaningful book*
> whose letters make manifest that which is concealed.
> (*Diwan*, 72.)

Imam 'Ali gives us another clue to his own nature and to the transformative impact of the Qur'an, what one might call its 'realisational power', in the following saying. He describes the recitation of the Qur'an as a process of infusing the quality of prophethood into the soul: 'For one who recites the Qur'an, it is as if prophethood is being woven into his very being (*fa-ka'annama udrijat al-nubuwwa bayna janbayhi*), except that he cannot be the recipient of the Revelation [i.e., cannot be regarded as a prophet in the strict sense].' The one who recites the Qur'an with his heart, and not just with his tongue, is thereby opening himself up to the theurgic power of the revealed speech fulgurating with the divine presence. It is as if he were being inwardly transformed into a prophetic being; but only one who receives the Revelation directly and immediately from God is a prophet in the full sense; all of those who receive the Revelation as mediated by the Prophet cannot therefore be qualified as prophets, hence the phrase *ka'annama*, 'as if'. This phrase comes again in a saying attributed to the Prophet: 'For one who recites a third of the Qur'an, it is as if he were given a third of prophethood; and he who recites two-thirds of the Qur'an, it is as if he were given two-thirds of prophethood; and he who recites the whole of the Qur'an, it is as if he were given the whole of prophethood.' Recitation of the revealed discourse is akin to imbibing from the celestial fountain whence the Revelation flows, and being inwardly transformed by this wine of divine Speech *into* the wine itself. As the great German mystic, Meister Eckhart (d. 1328), says in a different religious context, but with a metaphysical logic that applies whatever be the religious context: 'The bodily food we take is changed into us, but the spiritual food we receive changes us into itself' (Walshe, *Meister Eckhart*, 1:50). This spiritual transformation is wonderfully expressed by Imam 'Ali in the following esoteric saying:

> Truly, God has a drink for His friends (*awliya'ihi*). When they drink it, they are intoxicated (*sakaru*); and when they are intoxicated, they are enraptured (*tarabu*); and when they are enraptured, they are blessed (*tabu*); and when

they are blessed they dissolve (*dhabu*); and when they dissolve, they are free (*khalasu*); and when they are free, they devote themselves purely (*akhlasu*); and when they devote themselves purely, they seek (*talabu*); and when they seek, they find (*wajadu*); and when they find, they arrive (*wasalu*); and when they arrive, they are at one (*ittasalu*); there is no difference between them and their Beloved.

The mystical union being referred to here is the ultimate mystery, which is ineffable and inexpressible. As for union with the Qur'an, this relates to the process of becoming one with the *tajalli*, the theophanic self-manifestation, and not just self-disclosure, of the divine Reality. Rumi helps us to understand what this can mean.

> Ask about the meaning of the Qur'an from the Qur'an
>   alone;
>
> And from that one who has set fire to his desires;
>
> And has sacrificed himself to the Qur'an and is laid low;
>
> So that the Qur'an has become the essence of his spirit.
>
> The oil that has sacrificed itself totally to the rose—smell
>   either the oil or the rose: as you please!
>   (*Mathnawi*, 5: 3127–3130.)

Here, the distinction is drawn between the form of the human being—the 'oil'—and the essence of the Qur'anic spirit, the 'rose'. The person who has totally extinguished himself in the divine spirit of the Qur'an is described as one who has 'set fire to his desires,' a vivid description of the state of *fana*', extinction of selfhood. The scent of the oil is one with the scent of the rose: two different forms, but united by the same essence, the same fragrance—the same *baraka* ('blessing'), one might say. In one of the poems from his *Diwan*, Rumi pleads with us to enter into this state, and become one with the Qur'an:

> You love me, I'll make you perplexed, listen attentively!

Build less, as I ruin you, listen attentively!

If you build hundreds of cells like bees and ants,

I'll make you deserted, homeless and alone, listen attentively!

You endeavour that people, both men and women, may become dazzled by you,

I intend to dazzle and bewilder you, listen attentively!

...

Now, diminish your recitations, stay silent and have patience,

So that I may read and make you identical with the Qur'an, listen attentively!
(*Kulliyyat*, 5: 56–57, no.2204)

What, then, does it mean to become one with the Qur'an? Rumi gives this answer:

When you have fled (for refuge) to the Qur'an of God, you have mingled with the spirit of the prophets (*rawan-i anbiya'*).

The Qur'an is the states of the prophets (*hal-hay-yi anbiya'*), the fishes of the holy sea of (Divine) Majesty.
(*Mathnawi* 1:1537–1538).

According to Rumi, becoming identical to the Qur'an means, among other things, becoming one with 'the spirit' of all the prophets, and this implies assimilating *all* the states of consciousness of *all* of the prophets. It is, in other words, to become one with the *Haqiqa Muhammadiyya*, that spiritual reality of the Muhammadan substance to which the Prophet referred when he said that he was a prophet while Adam was still being moulded out of water and clay. This is the same reality to which Jesus refers when he said: 'Before Abraham was, I am' (John, 8:58): it is Jesus insofar as he is identified with the Logos, the 'Word', which was 'in the beginning' and 'from which all things were made' (see John, 1:1–3); just as the Prophet is describing himself insofar he is identified with that *Haqiqa* through which creation was manifested. Just as the Qur'an comprises the spiritual substance and states of consciousness of all previous prophets, so too does the Muhammadan Reality, the *batin* of *nubuwwa*, in other words: the *walaya*, emanating from God as *al-Wali*, and being manifested through all of God's 'friends', the prophets and the saints. Ibn 'Arabi affirms the same principle in a rather elliptical way, by saying that the spirit of the Qur'an manifests itself in form not only as the Book, but also as the man, Muhammad:

> He who—among the members of his community who did not live during his epoch— wishes to see Muhammad, let him look at the Qur'an. There is no difference between looking at it and looking at God's Messenger. It is as though the Qur'an had clothed itself in a form of flesh named Muhammad ibn 'Abd Allah ibn 'Abd al-Muttalib (Chodkiewiecz, *Seal*, 71).

If we note that the Prophet referred to 'Ali as being like his very self (*ka-nafsi*), it becomes easier to see the way in which the two selves are as one in their common spiritual substance, the *walaya* which, flowing from God, is divine and thus unique in its essence, while assuming infinitely diverse modes and degrees in the forms through which it traverses. The Prophet said to 'Ali: 'You are from me, and I am from you.' 'Ali is, quite evidently, 'from' the Prophet insofar as the immediate source of 'Ali's sanctity is the *walaya* coming from God through the Prophet. But the Prophet can also be seen as coming 'from' 'Ali if we appreciate that the Prophet is speaking symbolically: this is only insofar as 'Ali symbolises *walaya*, and he, the Prophet, symbolises *nubuwwa*, alone, without reference to the *walaya* that *nubuwwa* comprises at its heart. We are reminded here of the Prophet's famous designation of Fatima: *umm abiha*, 'the mother of her father.' For, even if the Prophet is always superior to the saint, in human terms, and the sanctity of the Prophet is always greater than the sanctity of the saint, nonetheless, the principle of *walaya* takes precedence over the principle of *nubuwwa*.

The relationships in question are more clearly seen when we recall that *al-Wali* is a name of God, whereas *al-Nabi* is not. In his *Fusus al-hikam*, Ibn 'Arabi makes this point, and tells us that sainthood is 'the encompassing, universal orbit, and this is why it does not end.' By contrast, 'law-giving prophethood and messengerhood, these do come to an end' (Dagli, *Ringstones*, 152). *Walaya* pertains to ultimate Reality, whereas *nubuwwa* is specific and time-bound, determined by the specific needs and imperatives attendant upon a particular legislative function in respect of a given community. The knowledge which defines the prophet's message, as prophet, is determined by the needs of his community. However, when a prophet expresses realities that fall outside the domain of the specific revealed Law (*shari'a*) with which he is sent, he does so in his capacity as 'a saint and a knower.' So his station as being a knower is 'more complete and more perfect' than his station as a lawgiving prophet. Therefore, what is meant by the claim that the saint is superior to the prophet is that this is so within 'a single individual' (Dagli, *Ringstones*, 153): the prophet's consciousness as a saint is superior to his consciousness as a prophet. This teaching comes through with particular clarity in the story of al-Khidr and Moses in the Surat al-Kahf ('The Cave', no. 18), to which we will be turning shortly.

In the light of these considerations, we may understand more deeply the meaning of the statement by Ibn 'Arabi, cited above: that 'Ali is 'imam of the world and the secret (*sirr*) of all the prophets' (*Futuhat* [1269/1853 ed.] 1:132); and Rumi's reference to Imam 'Ali as 'the pride of every prophet and every saint' (*Mathnawi*, 1:3723). All of the prophets take pride in 'Ali because he outwardly manifests the station of sanctity which at once transcends the station of their own prophethood, and defines the quintessence of their own inward reality. Let us note in this context another allusion to the mystery of Imam 'Ali, from a Persian commentary on one of the most important early manuals of Sufism, the *Kitab al-Ta'arruf li-madhhab ahl al-tasawwuf*, by Abu Bakr al-Kalabadhi (d. 990). The latter writes about the five founding fathers of Sufism: Imam 'Ali, his two sons, Imams Hasan and Husayn, then Imam 'Ali b. Husayn (Zayn al-'Abidin), and Imam Muhammad al-Baqir. In his commentary, Abu Ibrahim Mustamli Bukhari (d. 1042) says that 'Ali is 'the secret mystery of the gnostics (*sirr-i 'arifan*)'; and asserts that 'the whole Muslim community agree that he represents the breaths of inspiration of all the prophets (*anfas-i payghambaran*)' (cited in Lewisohn, *Ethics*, 113).

The following saying of the Prophet reveals—at least partially—the way in which Imam 'Ali can be seen as 'the pride of every prophet and every saint' and the 'secret of all the prophets':

> He who wishes to see Adam as regards his knowledge,
> Noah as regards his obedience,
> Abraham as regards his friendship [with God],
> Moses as regards his awe [of God], and
> Jesus as regards his purity:
> Let him look at 'Ali ibn Abi Talib.

Seeing Through the Lens of *Ta'wil*

The Prophet made a distinction between the *tanzil* of the Qur'an and its *ta'wil*. The latter concerns the esoteric interpretation of the revealed Book, disclosing its spiritual essence, while the former describes its 'descent', the revelation of the form of the Book, its outward, self-evident meaning. The

24

Prophet distinguished between *tanzil* and *ta'wil* in the following prediction: 'One of you will fight for the sake of the *ta'wil* of the Scripture, as I have fought for the sake of its *tanzil*.' He did not name 'Ali, but rather, in the spirit of *ta'wil* itself, made an allusion (*ishara*) to him. Various companions asked, one after the other, if he would be the one in question. The Prophet replied in the negative to each of them. Then he said that the person who would fight for the *ta'wil* of the Qur'an would be the one who was mending his sandals. At that moment, this was precisely what 'Ali was doing. As we shall see, this prophecy was fulfilled in more than one way.

The principle of *ta'wil* draws our consciousness towards the inner significance of Scripture, from the *zahir* (the 'outwardly apparent') to the *batin* (the 'inwardly hidden'). But this interiorisation of scriptural revelation presupposes a particular state of mind, an intuitive cognitive predisposition, whereby not only scripture but the whole of existence is 'interpreted' according to spiritual or archetypal principles. Our consciousness needs to be oriented from the world of particular phenomena and material facts to the domain of universal archetypes and spiritual symbols.

This shift of focus is alluded to in the following verse of the Qur'an: 'We shall show them Our signs on the horizons and in their own souls, until it be clear to them that He [or 'it'] is the Truth' (41:53). The Truth or the Real translates *al-Haqq*, one of the Names of God. As the great mystical philosopher Henry Corbin insisted, if we wish to perceive the spiritual reality of any phenomenon, we have to link outer, empirical perception to inner, spiritual consciousness. We need to read the 'signs' on the horizons of terrestrial geography as symbols of what resides in the spiritual topography of our own souls.

The notion of *ta'wil* takes us to the heart of the quest for the inner spiritual reality (*haqiqa*) of things, as the very root of the word, *awwala*, indicates: 'taking back to the beginning.' The beginning or origin of all things, *al-Awwal*,

25

'The First', is a Name of God. Looking at the past, in the spirit of *ta'wil*, is all about going back to the beginning, but it is also all about going to the end of all things. Both initiation and consummation are found in God: *al-Akhir*, 'The Last', is also a Name of God. For the spiritual processes of *ta'wil*, phenomena of the past and the future are contained in the inner space of the soul if our perspective on time is archetypal. That is, if we see history as a multi-layered stage upon which universal principles and archetypes manifest themselves rhythmically, rather than seeing history as a one-dimensional plane upon which isolated phenomena appear and disappear from moment to moment.

Imam 'Ali teaches us something about his own archetypal mystery in relation to Dhu'l-Qarnayn ('Possessor of two horns'), who is mentioned in the Surat al-Kahf ('The Cave'; see 18:83–98), often identified with Alexander the Great. When asked whether this person was a king or a prophet, Imam 'Ali replied in a manner that directs our attention away from the particularities of formal history and towards a universal archetype which manifests itself through different people in different times and places. First, he says that Dhu'l-Qarnayn was neither a king nor a prophet, but 'a slave who loved God and so was loved by God.' This is a double allusion to the archetype which he, Imam 'Ali, manifests. For the Prophet referred to 'Ali in just this way at the Battle of Khaybar (see Chapter 2), as one 'who loves God and His Messenger and is loved by God and His Messenger.' Secondly, it alludes to the principle of *walaya*: the *wali Allah* is the one who comes so close to God through voluntary devotions that God 'loves him'—this divine love investing and transfiguring all of the faculties and organs of the beloved devotee, as we saw above.

Then Imam 'Ali more directly refers to his own archetypal quality when he describes Dhu'l-Qarnayn as one who is raised up to his people, is struck by them 'on his right horn', and then placed by God into occultation for hundreds of years; raised

26

up again, struck by his people 'on his left horn', and then again placed into occultation for hundreds of years. The idea here is of a recurrent manifestation of an archetype, the function manifested taking priority over the person manifesting it, the universal archetype being more significant than its particular embodiment. Imam 'Ali then adds: 'and among you is one like him'—implying himself (see *Tafsir al-Qummi*, 2:15). One is reminded here of the Old Testament prophet Enoch (the Muslim 'Idris'), who, on account of being loved by God, was raised up into Heaven and did not die. Genesis tells us that Enoch did not die, but simply 'walked with God and he was no more, for God took him away' (Gen. 5:24). Enoch's profession was that of a cobbler who made and mended sandals (as noted by Amir-Moezzi, *Spirituality*, 320). It may not be a coincidence that, as noted above, when the Prophet designated the one who would 'fight for *ta'wil*,' he referred to 'Ali not by name, but as 'the one who is mending my sandals.' Also, it is noteworthy that the ascension of Enoch/Idris is described in the Qur'an as an ascent to an 'exalted place', the Arabic phrase here evoking the name of 'Ali: *makanan 'aliyyan* (19:57).

Imam 'Ali helps us to attune our sense of history (and of 'his story') to the supra-temporal domain of recurrent archetypes by referring to another prophetic figure who has the station of immortality: the prophet Elijah (in Greek, 'Elias'; in Arabic, 'Ilyas'). Imam 'Ali says, in one of his most esoteric discourses (entitled *Khutbat al-bayan*, 'the discourse which elucidates'): 'I am he who in the Gospel is called Elijah.' It is significant that he should have referred to the Gospel rather than the Old Testament, wherein Elijah figures in several places, most notably where he, like Enoch/Idris, is described as being taken directly to heaven without dying: '... there appeared a chariot of fire, and horses of fire... and Elijah went up by a whirlwind into heaven' (2 Kings 2:11). Like Enoch, then, Elijah is regarded in the Jewish tradition as immortal. It is prophesied that before the Final Judgement,

Elijah will come forth again: 'Behold, I will send you Elijah the prophet before the coming of the great and dreadful day of the Lord comes. He will turn the hearts of the parents to their children, and the hearts of the children to their parents; lest I strike the land with total destruction' (Malachi, 4:5–6).

In referring explicitly to the Gospel, however, and not the Old Testament, the Imam appears to be drawing our attention to the way in which Jesus refers to Elijah, identifying him with St John the Baptist. Jesus asks the people who they saw when they went to see John: 'A prophet? Yes, I say unto you, and more than a prophet. For this is he of whom it is written: "I will send my messenger before you, who will prepare your way before you." [paraphrasing Malachi, 3:1].... And if you are willing to accept it, he is the Elijah who was to come. Whoever has ears, let them hear' (Matthew, 11:9–15). Also in the Gospel of St Matthew we find the disciples, after witnessing the Transfiguration of Jesus on Mount Tabor (and witnessing Moses and Elijah by the side of Jesus), asking Jesus why the scribes of the scriptures say that Elijah must come before the Messiah. Jesus replies 'To be sure, Elijah comes and will restore all things. But I say unto you, Elijah has already come, and they did not recognise him.' The disciples then understood 'that he was talking to them about John the Baptist' (Matthew 17:10–13).

Jesus is clearly referring not to the individual prophet named Elijah, but to the spiritual function, the archetype which can be manifested through different individuals, in differing degrees of plenitude, and with differing accentuations of this or that facet of the archetype. One of the key aspects of the Elijah archetype is to prepare the way for the Messiah, which is precisely what St John the Baptist did in relation to Jesus, and what will be done by Elijah, 'the Tishbite' as he is called in Judaism, in relation to the Messiah still awaited by the Jews. Elijah paves the way for the Heavenly Peace to be inaugurated by the Messiah in the New Jerusalem (see Schaya,

28

'Mission of Elias'). But this is not the only spiritual function of Elijah.

According to Jewish tradition, he is the invisible, immortal spiritual master who continues to guide and inspire those seekers whose sincere thirst for God attracts the corresponding grace of realisatory power. His role in this respect is particularly accentuated within the mystical tradition of Judaism, the Kabbalah. Gershom Scholem tells us that the visions and revelations of Elijah (*gilluy Eliyahu*) are invoked at key points in the development of the Jewish mystical tradition. This tradition is therefore regarded not only as that which was transmitted on earth, but also as 'that which was received from the "celestial academy" above.' Scholem helps us to appreciate the scope and the subtlety of the ways in which Elijah operates (and let us note: in the Jewish tradition, Elijah is also regarded as an angel):

> The Prophet Elijah is for rabbinic Judaism the guardian of the sacred tradition. In the end, with the arrival of the Messiah, he will bring the divergent opinions of the teachers of the Torah into harmony. To the pious, he now reveals himself on diverse occasions in the marketplace, on the road, and at home... It is by no means the mystics alone who encounter him: he may just as well reveal himself to the simple Jew in distress as to one perfect in saintliness and learning (Scholem, *Origins of Kabbalah*, 35–36).

In order to help us see how this relates to Imam 'Ali, it would be useful to turn to one of Henry Corbin's great statements concerning the 'universal and liberating function of the active imagination':

> ...To typify, to transmute everything into an Image-symbol (*mithal*) by perceiving the correspondence between the hidden and the visible. And this typification (*tamthil*) of immaterial realities in the visible realities that

manifest them, accomplished by *ta'wil*, as the function par excellence of the Active Imagination, constitutes the renewal, the typological recurrence of similitudes (*tajdid al-muthul*), and that precisely is creation renewed and recurrent from instant to instant (*tajdid al-khalq*)... The symbolic exegesis that establishes typifications is creative in the sense that it transmutes things into symbols... and causes them to exist on another plane of being. To ignore this typology is to destroy the meaning of vision as such, and purely and simply to accept data as they present themselves in the raw (Corbin, *Creative Imagination*, 242–243).

Let us, then, use our 'active imagination' and engage in this process of typification (*tamthil*) in relation to Imam 'Ali. We may well arrive at a liberating vision of his archetype, that to which he appears to be alluding when he identifies himself, not simply with 'Elijah' but with 'he who in the Gospel is called Elijah,' thus, the archetypal figure who cannot be confined within any one religious framework. This archetype, which we can designate as '*Alawi* (pertaining to the quality personified by 'Ali), has many aspects, and corresponding functions, but at its heart is the function of sanctification through enlightenment. In other words, the individuals who manifest or personify this archetype impart spiritual initiation, guiding their disciples along the path to enlightenment. But the archetype does not only manifest its function through ordinary human intermediaries—imams, shaykhs, pirs, etc— through the regular channels of initiation and guidance. It also performs its work through the epiphany of sacred symbols and images, transmitted through spiritual visions, veridical dreams; or through the invisible casting of mystical intuitions, insights and openings; or through the awakening of the Truth already immanent in the heart—what the Imam referred to as 'unearthing the buried treasures of the intellect,' this being the essential function of all divine inspiration: enlightenment of the heart through the remembrance of God: 'God is the *Wali* of those who believe. He brings them forth from the darknesses into the Light' (Q 2:257). With the help of our 'active imagination', we can see without difficulty that this *'Alawi* function, flowing from and manifesting the divine Name, *al-Wali*, transcends the boundaries of Islam, and is universal in its scope—as the Imam's explicit self-identification with 'he who in the Gospel is called Elijah' makes clear.

At the Transfiguration of Jesus, briefly mentioned above, the Gospel tells us that Moses and Elijah were present. This is significant. For, according to the Kabbalah, these two figures are representative of the distinction between the exoteric and the esoteric. Moses is the Lawgiver, Elijah the Spiritual Guide. When we note that, in the Islamic tradition, the figure of Elijah (Ilyas) is identified with al-Khidr, to the point that they are seen as the same individual (as Louis Massignon noted in a seminal article, 'Élie et son role transhistorique', 269), we are taken back to the Surat al-Kahf, where the distinction between the esoteric and the exoteric, the *batin* and the *zahir*, is given its most explicit expression. At the heart of this chapter is the dramatic confrontation between Moses and 'one of Our slaves, unto whom We have given mercy from Ourselves, and knowledge from Our presence *(min ladunna)*' (18:65). This 'slave' is identified by Muslim tradition with al-Khidr, and, as noted above, the latter is in turn identified with Elias—we are clearly in the presence of the *'Alawi* archetype.

The story, in brief, of the encounter between Moses and al-Khidr is as follows: Moses, accompanied by his servant, is searching for the confluence of 'the two rivers' (symbolising the 'Waters of Life' or *Fons vitae*, the fountain of immortality). He comes upon al-Khidr and seeks to accompany this personage in order to learn from him. Moses is accepted on condition that he not question any of the actions of his teacher. After being bewildered by three apparently unlawful or inappropriate acts committed by his master,

Moses remonstrates with him, and is then shown the divine purpose underlying each of the the the acts. Al-Khidr says to him finally: 'This is the *ta'wil* of that which you had not the patience to bear' (18:60–82). Moses is thus taught the science of *ta'wil*, by means of which the outward, *al-zahir*, is retraced to its inward reality, *al-batin*.

All of this is clearly bound up with the essence of *walaya*, and it should be noted that the word *walaya*, in this form, comes only once in the whole of the Qur'an, in this very chapter (18:44). One of the central messages of this chapter is, precisely, the superiority of *walaya* vis-à-vis *nubuwwa*. But, as Ibn 'Arabi points out, the whole drama of the encounter between the guiding saint and the lawgiving prophet is to be seen as unfolding within the soul of Moses. In this microcosmic interpretation, al-Khidr symbolises a degree of consciousness within the heart of Moses: 'He [al-Khidr] showed him [Moses] nothing but his own form; so it was his own state that he beheld, his own soul with which he remonstrated' (Gril, 342). In other words, the 'al-Khidr' of Moses' being is that element of his own consciousness which transcends the formal limitations attendant upon the specific ordinances of religious law. We return to the fundamental theme: *walaya* is the quintessence of *nubuwwa*.

Understood thus, this chapter shows us the subtlety of the relationship between *walaya* and *ta'wil*, and helps us to appreciate that the 'methodology' of *ta'wil*, as taught by al-Khidr to Moses, is not just about the esoteric interpretation of scripture: it is also, and perhaps more fundamentally, about the esoteric understanding of events, phenomena, 'scriptural' signs all around us and, most importantly of all, within us. Let us repeat: 'We shall show them Our signs on the horizons and in their own souls' (Q 41:53).

This is the kind of *ta'wil* that the prophet Joseph is taught, according to the chapter named after him, Chapter 12. His father, Jacob, says to him, after hearing of Joseph's dream:

'Your Lord has chosen you, and will teach you the *ta'wil* of events (*ahadith*)' (12:6). In the same chapter, after Joseph has been sold into slavery in Egypt, God declares: 'Thus We established Joseph in the land, that We might teach him the *ta'wil* of events' (12:21). And again, after Joseph declares that the prostration of his parents and his brothers to him is the fulfilment of his dream—or rather, it is 'the *ta'wil* of my dream of old' (12:100)—he shows us that *ta'wil* is not restricted to dream interpretation or scriptural interpretation. For he repeats the phrase, which now comes for the third time in this chapter: 'O my Lord, You have given me [a part] of sovereignty, and You have taught me the *ta'wil* of events,' and he adds this allusion to the relationship between *ta'wil* and *walaya*: 'You are my *Wali* in the world and in the Hereafter' (12:101).

We can conclude this discussion of *ta'wil* with the following extract from Rumi's *Mathnawi*. It helps us grasp the difference between historicism—in which empirical facts of history are reified, seen as 'data' pertaining only to the past—and the 'transhistorical' perspective that is created by a vision of the perpetually present realm of spiritual archetypes, the kind of vision opened up by Imam 'Ali's teachings. In the middle of one of his stories concerning Moses and Pharaoh in Book 3 of the *Mathnawi*, Rumi suddenly breaks off the narrative and speaks directly to his readers—in what might be interpreted, in modern parlance, as the poet's own 'deconstruction' of the 'reifying' processes of thought in his readers' minds:

> The mention of Moses has become a chain to the thoughts (of my readers), for (they think) that these are stories which happened long ago. The mention of Moses serves for a mask, but the light of Moses is thy actual concern, O good man. Moses and Pharaoh are in thy being: thou must seek these two adversaries in thyself. The (process) of generation from Moses is (continuing) till the

33

Resurrection: the Light is not different (though) the lamp
has become different (*Mathnawi*, 3:1251–1255).

◆

In the chapters that follow, we will try to view the life of Imam
'Ali, a 'perfect human being', through the lens of *ta'wil*. We
hope to glimpse thereby something of the *haqiqa*, or spiritual
reality, of the person who, as we noted in the Introduction,
was designated by the Prophet as the 'gate' to prophetic
consciousness; that is, consciousness of the *Haqiqa* as such,
the ultimate Reality, revealed to and through the Prophet.
This book aims to demonstrate that Imam 'Ali opens the gate
of prophetic wisdom, here and now, for each and every one
of us, through his wisdom; and also by showing us, among
other things, how a perfect human being inwardly overcame
a far-from-perfect world. After the Prophet's death, Imam 'Ali
lived a quiet life, far from the political domain, teaching all
those who came to him for guidance, including each of the
three rulers of the Muslim community who preceded him.
Then, after around twenty-five years of life as an imam, that
is, as a spiritual guide, he became caliph, the ruler of an
immense empire. As head of state he initiated a series of major
reforms of Muslim society, even while being pre-occupied by
the appalling civil wars precipitated by rebellions against his
rule. Tragically, his efforts to reform the corruptions inherited
from the previous regime were thwarted by the sword of the
assassin, after just four and a half years of rule.

Nonetheless, the wisdom expressed through his sayings,
and embodied in his actions and intentions, remain permanently accessible to those 'with ears to hear': those whose hearts
are, to whatever degree, attuned to the remembrance of God.
They will find that the degree of perfection attained by Imam
'Ali—a reflection of the perfection of the Prophet himself—is
not something metaphysically incomprehensible and ethically
unattainable. For Imam 'Ali manifested his sanctity in ways

that are intelligible to all: his mystical teaching and chivalrous virtue went hand in hand with what the Qur'an calls 'small acts of kindness':

> Do you see the person who denies the religion? He is the one who repels the orphan, and does not exhort people to feed the poor. So woe be to the worshippers! Those who neglect [to do what is required by] their worship; those who are only showing off; and refuse small acts of kindness (107:1–7).

Imam 'Ali was famous for 'small acts of kindness' throughout his life, and these acts became particularly well known when he was caliph: he would very often travel alone, in disguise, through his domains, performing whatever acts of charity he could, without the beneficiary of his charity knowing who he was. The sources abound with anecdotes of his kindness, but the following will suffice. Towards the end of his caliphate, after the Battle of Nahrawan against the Kharijites (see Chapter 3), he came across a woman who was struggling with a heavy load. He helped her with it, carrying it to her home. In the course of conversation, he discovered that she was a widow, whose husband was a Kharijite who had been killed by Imam 'Ali's army at Nahrawan. He also saw how difficult it was for her to meet the daily needs of her orphaned children. She severely criticised the caliph, without knowing that the man helping her was none other than the caliph himself. The following day, Imam 'Ali returned to her with a bag full of food, and engaged in conversation with her children affectionately while lighting the fire for the widow. A neighbour came in, and when he recognised the caliph he remonstrated with the widow for the way she was speaking to the 'Commander of the Faithful'. She fell to the ground, begging for forgiveness. Imam 'Ali said: 'It is 'Ali who must feel ashamed at having neglected you' (Lalljee, 227–228). As we shall see in Chapter 3, one of Imam 'Ali's highest priorities as ruler was to provide for the poor, the aged, the widows, the orphans, the disabled and prisoners of war. During his caliphate, 'small acts of kindness' were writ large as a policy, or rather, as an imperative moral obligation of the state towards all those in dire need of assistance.

The sources are replete with such stories. They serve an extremely important function, for they illustrate how the loftiest truths of the Spirit go hand in hand with 'small acts of kindness' which are well within our reach. If we do not perform acts of kindness, as the Qur'an tells us, our acts of religious devotion are nothing but show, and we are guilty of 'denying' Islam. When, however, religious devotion is accompanied by kindness, and all the virtues mentioned above, then not only is the religion of Islam properly upheld, but also, the texture of our intelligence is immeasurably enriched. We begin to assimilate the truth with our heart, rather than just our mind; the deeper realities of faith, referred to by Imam ʿAli as *haqa'iq al-iman*, begin to unfold for us. We start understanding, with the heart, the deeper teachings of the religion; and we are initiated into the process by which ordinary belief becomes heartfelt faith, faith becomes unshakeable certainty, and certainty becomes liberating gnosis (*maʿrifa*).

2

In the Footsteps of the Prophet

Imam 'Ali had the extraordinary distinction of being born within the Ka'ba itself. A wide variety of historical sources attest to this fact (see, for a discussion of these sources, Pakatchi, *Mawlid*). Some of them contain descriptions of the miraculous way in which the doors of the Ka'ba were opened, but all agree that his mother, Fatima bint Asad, gave birth to him within the Ka'ba's walls. According to one report, she invoked the name of her ancestor Abraham in her supplication to God just before her son was born: 'I believe that my ancestor, Abraham, was the builder of the Ka'ba... and I implore Thee, by the right of the one by whom this Holy House was built, and by the right of the one who is in my womb, to make easy my labour.'

The very beginning of Imam 'Ali's history, then, already evokes something of a timeless mystery, for his birth in the house of worship built by his ancestor Abraham, through the line of Ishmael, symbolically heralds a deep and intimate relationship between Imam 'Ali and the generations of men and women following faithfully in the steps of Abraham. They were known as the *hunafa'* (singular *hanif*), individuals who remained true to Abrahamic monotheism, and who are thus referred to in the Qur'an as *muslim*, in the literal rather than confessional sense, that is: in a state of submission to God. The *hanif* is thus a 'Muslim' in the sense of adhering to primordial monotheism (*tawhid*) even before the advent of the formal religion of Islam brought by the Prophet Muhammad. As the Qur'an says, indicating the way in which Abraham's faith both precedes and transcends the confessional labels which monotheism came to assume in later centuries: 'Abraham was not a Jew, nor a Christian; rather, he was a *hanif*, a *muslim*' (3:67).

'Ali was born when the Prophet was about thirty years old; in other words, roughly ten years before the latter's prophetic mission began. When he was around six years old, 'Ali was taken into the Prophet's household. Abu Talib, 'Ali's father, was Muhammad's paternal uncle, brother of Muhammad's father 'Abdallah. But Abu Talib was regarded by Muhammad as being more of a father than an uncle. Muhammad had lost his own father before he was born, and he soon lost his mother, and then his grandfather, 'Abd al-Muttalib, who had taken charge of the orphan. At this point, Abu Talib assumed responsibility for Muhammad's upbringing; the relationship between the two was very close, and the Prophet never forgot the kindness and generosity that Abu Talib showed him throughout his formative years. Therefore, when Abu Talib found himself struggling during a famine in Mecca, Muhammad had no hesitation in offering to relieve his uncle's burden by taking one of his sons, 'Ali, from him, and bringing him up in his own household. Thus began an intimate relationship between Muhammad and 'Ali, more akin to father and son than first cousins. As Imam 'Ali says in one of his sermons, as recorded in the *Nahj al-balagha* (in the sermon known as *al-Qasi'a*):

> When I was but a child he took me under his wing... I would follow him [the Prophet] as a baby camel follows the footsteps of its mother. Every day he would raise up for me a sign of his noble character, commanding me to follow it. He would go each year into seclusion at [the mountain of] Hira'. I saw him and nobody else saw him. At that time no household was brought together for the

religion of Islam, except [that comprising] the Messenger of God, Khadija [the wife of the Prophet] and myself as the third. I saw the light of the Revelation and the message, and I smelt the fragrance of prophecy...

'Ali had the inestimable privilege of accompanying the Prophet on his spiritual retreats—at least once, according to the words above. It is likely that 'Ali took provisions to the Prophet, as these retreats could last for over a month. It was during one of these retreats that Muhammad received the first revelation (96:1-5). It is recorded in the sources that the Prophet regularly went into seclusion during the month of Ramadan in the years preceding the descent of the Qur'an. In his commentary on the above sermon, Ibn Abi'l-Hadid (*Sharh*, 13:210) refers to reports that 'Ali regularly accompanied the Prophet on his retreats. According to one of these, by Imam Ja'far al-Sadiq, both the Prophet and 'Ali heard and saw phenomena which were subsequently interpreted to be the foreshadowings of revelations, and it was on one of these retreats that the angel Gabriel first appeared to the Prophet. The Prophet is reported to have said to 'Ali: 'If I were not the seal of the prophets, you would have a share in prophecy; but, even though you are not a prophet, you are the *wasi* (legatee) and the *warith* (heir) of a prophet. Indeed, you are the lord of legatees (*sayyid al-awsiya'*) and leader of the pious (*imam al-atqiya'*).'

This accords with what the Prophet said to Imam 'Ali, recounted by the latter in the sermon *al-Qasi'a*: 'You hear what I hear, and you see what I see; but you are not a *nabi* (prophet). Rather, you are a *wazir* (vicegerent)...' It can be concluded from these statements that, although 'Ali was not a prophet, he had been granted a high spiritual station even as a youth. 'Ali sees 'the light of revelation' which we can understand as the spiritual light radiating from the revelation, and which can also mean the light emanating from the Prophet during his states of consciousness when receiving the revelation in all its plenitude. When Imam 'Ali claims to have smelt the 'fragrance of prophecy', this is not to be confused with directly receiving prophecy; the 'fragrance' of prophecy is one thing, prophecy as such, another: 'Ali was a saint—indeed, a saint of the highest order—but not a prophet. The Prophet said to him: 'The relationship between you and me is akin to that between Aaron and Moses, except that after me there will be no prophet.'

The First Muslim after the Prophet?

Imam 'Ali's statement about praying with the Prophet and Khadija at a time when nobody else was praying according to the newly revealed rites brings us to the important and contested question of his *sabiqa*, 'precedence', in embracing Islam. 'Ali is described in the standard biography of the Prophet, that of Ibn Ishaq, as 'the first male to believe in the apostle of God, to pray with him and to believe in his divine message, when he was a boy of ten' (Guillaume, *Life of Muhammad*, 114). According to accounts given by various authorities, the Prophet received his mission on a Monday, and the following day 'Ali affirmed his belief in his message (Suyuti, *History*, 171).

The historic moment when 'Ali's Islam was made public came after the Prophet received the command to declare his mission to his near kin (Q 26:214). He accordingly summoned 'Ali, who was then still a youth of about thirteen, and told him to invite the clan of 'Abd al-Muttalib to hear his message and to prepare a meal for them. 'Ali did as he was instructed. However, before the Prophet could speak, it is reported that Abu Lahab, one of his uncles, told the clan to disperse, saying that Muhammad had placed a spell on them; the small amount of food and drink that had been prepared seemed not to diminish, however much the guests ate. The Prophet told 'Ali to invite the clan to return the following day, and before Abu Lahab could intervene he addressed them as follows: 'O clan of Banu 'Abd al-Muttalib, I know of no man among the Arabs who has brought his people something better than what I have brought to you. I bring you the best of this world and the next, for God has commanded me to summon you to Him. Which of you will aid me in this matter, so that he will be my brother, my heir (*wasi*) and my successor (*khalifa*) among you?' In his own narration of this event, reported by al-Tabari, 'Ali recounts:

> They all held back, and although I was the youngest, I said: 'I will be your helper, Prophet of God.' He put his hand on the back of my neck and said, 'This is my brother, my heir, and my successor among you, so listen to him and obey him.' They rose up laughing [and saying to Abu Talib], 'He has commanded you to listen to your son and to obey him!'

From the Sunni point of view, the Prophet's words are not taken as a designation (*nass*) of 'Ali as his successor in political terms—even though the term *khalifa* was used in his statement. From the Shi'i point of view, the Prophet's words are taken literally, as evidence that the Prophet did indeed designate 'Ali as his successor. Between these two points of view, considered on the political plane, there appears to be no possible compromise. However, it is possible to surpass the plane of politics, and to interpret the statement of the Prophet in terms of spiritual authority, thus reconciling the two viewpoints. We will return to this question below, in our discussion of the Ghadir Khumm *hadith*. What is indisputable is that 'Ali inherited from the Prophet a treasure of inestimable spiritual value, the inheritance in question being *walaya*, the essential meaning of which, as we have seen, is sanctity, initiatic power, sanctified authority, affiliation and love. The debate between Shi'is and Sunnis hinges on the question of whether this *walaya* also connotes political power.

41

There is no debate, however, concerning the fact that 'Ali was the first male—despite his age—to embrace Islam, Khadija being the first woman to do so, and Abu Bakr the first adult male. The question of 'Ali's age at the time he embraced Islam, and at the time he was described as brother, executor and successor of the Prophet, became central to later debates between Shi'is and Sunnis over the issue of 'precedence' (*sabiqa*) in embracing Islam, especially in relation to Abu Bakr. Some Sunni scholars, such as Jahiz, in their effort to raise the status of Abu Bakr above that of 'Ali, regard 'Ali as not yet having attained maturity (*bulugh*) at the time he embraced the new faith. Shi'i scholars, on the other hand, such as Ibn Shahrashub, retort that 'Ali's youth is to be viewed as one of his great merits. They argue that it brings 'Ali into the same category of spiritual maturity as that of John the Baptist (in Arabic, 'Yahya') who, according to the Qur'an, was 'given wisdom when still a child' (19:12); and even of Jesus, who is described as miraculously speaking as a baby from the cradle (19:30) (Ibn Shahrashub, 2:17).

Hijra

When the Prophet decided to migrate to Medina, together with his small community of persecuted Muslims, he asked 'Ali to perform an important role which would enable him to escape from the city unharmed. He had come to learn that the Quraysh were planning to assassinate him; one young man from each clan had been chosen to participate in the assassination, so that the responsibility for the act would be shared. The Prophet asked 'Ali if he would be willing to sleep in his bed, pretending to be him, knowing that the Quraysh were spying on him that very night, intending to kill him in the morning. 'Ali replied by asking whether the Prophet would be safe if he, 'Ali, did what was asked of him.

Upon being assured by the Prophet that he would indeed be safe, 'Ali performed a ritual prostration to God out of gratitude, and then told the Prophet that he was willing to sacrifice his life for the sake of the Prophet's safety. 'Ali slept that night in the Prophet's bed, and when he was discovered there in the morning, the enraged Qurayshis realised their plan had been thwarted. It is in relation to this episode that verse 2:207 was said to have been revealed: 'And there is the type of man who sells his life to earn the good pleasure of God.' This incident reveals a central aspect of 'Ali's character: absolute fearlessness. It teaches us that where there is absolute faith, there will be an equally absolute courage: fearing nothing but the Absolute means being empowered with absolute fearlessness. This is a key to understanding Imam 'Ali's courage. Charles Upton cites a saying of the Imam: 'Courage and Truth are always found together—like falsehood and cowardice,' and provides another key for helping us to see the relationship between faith—belief in the absolute Truth—and courage, by reminding us that, according to its etymology, courage is rooted in the heart, *cor*, in Latin (Upton, 52–55). So the lesson taught to us by the bravery manifested by Imam 'Ali as a youth is that believing in the Truth, with all one's heart, will always result in true courage. Conversely, absence of faith in the Truth generates fear and cowardice.

Medina

The first significant event to take place in Medina in relation to 'Ali was his ceremonial naming as the 'brother' of the Prophet. This pact of 'brothering' (*ukhuwwa*) was proposed by the Prophet as a means of cementing the new Muslim community, symbolically indicating that the bond of faith transcended the ties of blood. Approximately 90 men were reported to have entered into this 'brotherhood', the Prophet indicating to each man the person who was henceforth to be regarded as his brother. When the men, each one of the Meccan 'Emigrants' (*al-muhajirun*) being paired to one of the Medinan Muslims, the 'Helpers' (*al-ansar*), 'Ali was the last person to be 'brothered', and asked the Prophet: 'You have appointed a brother to everyone here, and I alone am left, so who will be my brother?' The Prophet said: 'By Him who raised me up with truth as a prophet, I have not left you out but for the sake of myself: the relationship between you and me is akin to that between Aaron and Moses, except that after me there will be no prophet.' Then the Prophet recited words from verse 15:47, 'brothers upon thrones, face to face.' As we shall see in the following chapter, 'Ali cites this verse, as caliph after a civil war, in a most unexpected way.

One of the greatest honours accorded to 'Ali in this early Medinan period was his marriage to the Prophet's daughter, Fatima. Other leading companions had sought her hand, but the Prophet had refused each one of them, saying that her marriage was to be determined not by human choice but divine inspiration. It was only when 'Ali made his proposal that the Prophet accepted, saying that the marriage tie between the two had been made in Paradise. The marriage took place in the second year of the Hijra (623). The Prophet told Fatima she was marrying a leader both of this world and the next; the first of his companions to drink from the *hawd* (a pool or fountain in Paradise) would be the first among them who affirmed faith in his message—and he was the person whom she was marrying.

There is a mystical significance here. For the *hawd* is identifiable with the fountain in Paradise named 'Kawthar' in the Qur'an, and this fountain is symbolically related to the personage of Fatima (see the Qur'anic chapter 'Al-Kawthar', no. 108). The word itself means 'abundance', and it is understood by the commentators to mean both the abundance of grace that was to pass through Fatima (that is, the Prophet's progeny, all the 'sayyids', or 'lords' of the community) and also the celestial abundance promised to the Prophet in Paradise, neither meaning excluding the other. The mysticism here is deepened when we take into account 'Ali's designation as the 'Cupbearer of Kawthar' (*saqi al-kawthar*) in reference to his function of bringing celestial wine into this world from the fountain of Kawthar (see 76:5–6), which is expressed in physical terms by his being the husband of Fatima, and forebear of all of the Prophet's progeny through her.

The great Persian poet, Hafiz, refers to this designation in the following verse of poetry. Here, he does not mention 'Ali by name, but alludes to him through his acts and traits, a rhetorical device which highlights the spiritual qualities that made Imam 'Ali who he was. The servant of the Imam, Qanbar, is referred to as Khwajah, 'lord', thus elevating even higher the station of the one who was the master of this 'lord':

> For manliness, ask the uprooter of the Khaybar gate [i.e., 'Ali];
>
> For the mysteries of magnanimity, ask Khwajah Qanbar [about his master, 'Ali].
>
> Do you truly seek the graceful effusion of the Real, Hafiz?
>
> Ask its wellspring, the cupbearer of Kawthar.
> (*Ruba'i* no.22)

Similarly, Farid al-Din 'Attar, in the prologue to his unsurpassable monument of Persian poetry, *Mantiq al-tayr* ('Language of the Birds'), refers to Imam 'Ali as *saqi-i Kawthar*; and also as 'the mountain of forbearance (*kuh-i hilm*)', 'the gate of knowledge (*bab-i 'ilm*)', 'the pole of religion (*qutb-i din*)', and 'the impeccable lord (*khwaja-i ma'sum*)', among several other such honorific titles ('Attar, *Mantiq al-tayr*, 53).

♦

45

Another honour accorded to 'Ali by the Prophet was that, when the congregational mosque was built, all doors leading into the mosque from the various small homes (or apartments) that surrounded it were to be closed up, except his. This instruction, according to the Prophet, was divinely inspired: 'God Almighty commanded unto me that all the doors which opened onto the mosque must be closed except the door of 'Ali's house. I never make orders myself that doors must be closed or be kept open. In such matters I follow the command of God.' Here, we cannot help seeing enacted one outward dimension of the profound symbolism expressed by the Prophet, as noted earlier: 'I am the city of knowledge,' said the Prophet, 'and 'Ali is its gate.'

La Fata Illa 'Ali:
No Chivalric Youth But 'Ali

As has already been seen, 'Ali's dedication to God and the Prophet was imbued with fearless courage. He was to acquire a reputation in Islamic tradition not only as an invincible warrior but also as the very archetype of the chivalric knight. He was deemed 'invincible' in that he was in fact never defeated in any of the single-combat duels (al-biraz), or in any general battle in which he fought. His chivalry was demonstrated by the stress he always placed on fighting only in self-defence, on the one hand, and by the magnanimity he manifested towards his defeated foes, on the other. This latter aspect is particularly striking (as we shall see in the following chapter) at the Battle of the Camel, in his attitude towards 'Aisha, and also to Talha and Zubayr.

The foundation for 'Ali's reputation as a warrior was established in the first battle fought by the Muslims at Badr, when the nascent Muslim army was confronted by an army of Quraysh three times its size. Permission to resort to warfare, in self-defence, had been given by what most commentators claim to be the very first revelation pertaining to warfare: 'Permission [to fight] is granted to those who are being fought against, for they have been oppressed...' (22:39–40).

At this battle, which took place during the month of Ramadan (2/624), around seventy poorly equipped Muslims confronted an army of over two hundred well-equipped Quraysh. At the outset of the battle, three of the champions of the Quraysh came out to meet three Muslims. Walid b. Utba challenged 'Ali to single combat and was defeated by him. At the second battle, at Uhud (3/625), 'Ali accepted the challenge issued by Talha b. Talha, and defeated him. It was in the course of this battle that 'Ali acquired the title *fata*, 'chivalric youth'. Although the outcome of the battle was indecisive, 'Ali's valour and personal victories were recorded. He was sent by the Prophet to fight various groups of the Quraysh, and returned, having defeated them all. The Prophet made the following statement: 'Verily 'Ali is of me and I am of 'Ali.' It is reported that the voice of Gabriel was then heard, saying: 'And I am of both of you.' Then a voice from heaven was heard to proclaim: 'There is no sword but Dhu'l-Faqar and no chivalric youth but 'Ali.'

As we shall see below, in 'Ali's conduct in battle when he was caliph, his designation as the archetypal knight implied much more than simply his martial prowess: his spiritual chivalry was all about mastery of oneself and mercy to others. This is made clear in a revealing narrative in Rumi's *Mathnawi*. It is based on a historical incident at the Battle of the Trench (Khandaq) in 5/627. 'Ali was challenged to a duel by 'Amr b. Abd Wudd, a giant of a man, the most fearsome champion in the ranks of the soldiers arrayed against the Muslims in this, the third of the major military encounters between the Muslims and the Quraysh. 'Amr crossed the trench separating the two armies, and challenged a single man to come forward to fight him. 'Ali was allowed by the Prophet to go forth.

He defeated 'Amr, but not before the following incident took place. Having disarmed his opponent, 'Ali was seen to hesitate, as if in fear. Later, he explained why he had drawn back: 'He had reviled my mother and spat in my face. I feared that if I struck then, it would have been out of personal anger. So I left him until I had calmed down.' A greater contrast between today's fanatical 'jihadists' and this true knight of Islam is difficult to imagine.

This incident was immortalised by Rumi, who shares with us a vision of the spiritual essence of what transpired in that moment when 'Ali refused to kill 'Amr. The vision of 'Ali is in fact a most revealing picture of the archetypal knight of Islam, a picture which evokes the total self-mastery and the detachment, the dispassion and the sense of transcendence, associated with the ideal Zen warrior in the Japanese Bushido tradition. For a split second, 'Ali was brought out of his state of dispassionate composure, when the face that we are supposed to contemplate with reverence was instead besmirched with defiance.

> Learn how to act sincerely from 'Ali: know that the Lion
>   of God was purged of all deceit.
>
> In fighting against the infidels he got the upper hand
>   of a certain knight, and quickly drew a sword and
>   made haste [to slay him].
>
> He [Abd al-Wudd] spat on the face of 'Ali, the pride of
>   every prophet and every saint.
>
> He spat on the countenance before which the face of the
>   moon bows low in the place of worship.
>   (*Mathnawi*, 1:3721–3724)

The narrative continues for several pages, in the course of which many subtle teachings are given, which can be summed up by the line with which the entire narrative begins: 'learn how to act sincerely from 'Ali.' Sincerity (*ikhlas*) can also be translated as 'purity': 'Ali's actions were 'purely' for God, with no trace of egotistic motivation. 'I have removed the baggage of self out of the way, I have deemed [what is] other than God to be non-existence,' he says, (*Mathnawi*, 1:3790). Having removed the 'baggage' of the self, what flows from him are the divine Names and Qualities, and for this reason he is described by Rumi as 'all mind and eye' (1:3745), or all intellect and vision. For where the distorting lens of the ego is absent, the vision of the intellect is total, complete, seeing without any interference the beauty and reality of the divine Names and Qualities.

We should note another insight from Rumi's inspired vision: 'Anger is king over kings, and to me it is a slave,' 'Ali says, 'even anger I have bound under the bridle. The sword of my forbearance has smitten the neck of my anger' (*Mathnawi*, 1:3799–3800). This is extremely important if we wish to understand not just the chivalric ethic of *futuwwa* which 'Ali personified to perfection—an ethic which became institutionalised, in his name, throughout the medieval period in the Muslim world—but also the very nature of *jihad* in Islam.

Contrary to what contemporary 'jihadists' do and say, the authentic Muslim knight is one whose forbearance (*hilm*) has 'smitten the neck' of his anger. The virtue of *hilm* is central to what we have called elsewhere the 'prophetic paradigm' (see Shah-Kazemi, *Tolerance*, 111–130). *Hilm* is not only forbearance, gentleness and composure but also self-control, self-mastery and, in its highest expression, self-transcendence, together with the wisdom that flows from such qualities. So central is this character trait that the Prophet described the *halim*, one possessing the quality of *hilm*, as follows: 'The *halim*,' he said, 'is almost a prophet.' In contrast, anger destroys good deeds 'as fire consumes wood,' according to the Prophet. As we shall see in the following chapter, 'Ali advises his newly appointed governor of Egypt, Malik al-Ashtar, to choose as head of the army a man who has the following characteristics: 'the purest of heart, the one most excellent in forbearance (*hilm*); who is slow to anger, happy to pardon, kind to the weak, severe with the strong; one who is neither moved by violence, nor held back by weakness.' One who loses his temper, resorts quickly to violence and has no self-control is not to be regarded as a true warrior, still less trusted as an army commander. As 'Ali puts it simply: 'The intelligence of one who cannot control his anger will always be incomplete.'

Here, let us note that another great Sufi, Abu Hamid al-Ghazali, also cites the incident concerning 'Amr, using it to teach us that egotism in all its manifestations, and most especially fanaticism (*ta'assub*), must be overcome as a condition for practising the Qur'anic principle of 'enjoining the good and forbidding evil' (*al-amr bi'l-ma'ruf wa'l-nahy 'an al-munkar*; al-Ghazali, *Kimiya'*, 1:517). In other words, the true warrior is one whose actions flow from self-mastery: indeed, al-Ghazali refers to mastery over one's ego as the key to spiritual happiness; by contrast, being mastered by one's ego is the essence of wretchedness (al-Ghazali, *Disciplining the Soul*, 122). Fanaticism and rage—giving in to the lowest parts of one's ego—are the very antithesis of the dispassion and generosity which must motivate the Muslim knight, who fights only in self-defence, and always with a profound sense of regret: 'Never seek a fight with your enemy,' said the Prophet; and the Qur'an says: 'Fighting is incumbent upon you, even though it is hateful to you' (2:216). Echoing this, Imam 'Ali said, in the letter to Malik just cited, 'Never reject any call to peace made to you by your enemy.' In one of his most famous pieces of advice to his son al-Hasan, cited as one of his aphorisms in the *Nahj al-balagha*, he said: 'Do not call people to fight; but if you are challenged to fight, then accept. Truly the one who calls others to fight is an oppressive rebel (*baghi*), and an oppressive rebel is one who will inevitably be laid low.' All of Imam 'Ali's feats on the field of battle are to be seen in this light: with complete self-mastery, and without a hint of personal anger, let alone rage, he took up arms in self-defence, for the sake of the Truth, and in pursuit of justice; he did so reluctantly but courageously, with both compassion and dispassion.

At the Battle of Khaybar (7/629), 'Ali's reputation as a warrior came to assume legendary proportions. To this day, one of his epithets in the Persianate world and the Indian subcontinent is 'breaker of Khaybar' (*khaybar-shekan*). The Muslims were unable to make any headway against the strong fortresses of the Jews at Khaybar. The Prophet then declared that he would give the banner of his army to a man 'who loves God and His Messenger and is loved by God and His Messenger'—an allusion to the mystery of *walaya*, as discussed in Chapter 1. He predicted that victory would be granted by God to the Muslims through this person.

He then sent for 'Ali, who first had to accept a challenge from the champion of the Jewish army, Marhab. Defeating Marhab in single combat, he went on to lead the charge against the fortresses, which resulted in victory for the Muslims. Legends about his superhuman strength abounded: witnesses claimed that in the heat of the battle he ripped a massive gate from its hinges and used it as a shield, a gate which afterwards needed seven men to lift it up.

It was probably after this event that 'Ali's fame spread far and wide, to the point that some went so far as to divinize him, claiming that only God could have lifted and used such a heavy gate as a shield. Needless to say, 'Ali gave such people short shrift: there are accounts that he severely remonstrated with, even punished, those who asserted his divinity. He was aware, as were the intelligent companions of the Prophet, that it was not the power of the man, 'Ali ibn Abi Talib, that was responsible for this feat: it was the power of God alone, working through the man. 'There is no power or strength except by God': this formula, taught by the Prophet, summed up Muslim belief on this important point. It is the formula which corresponds most closely to the words of Christ: 'With men, this is impossible, but with God all things are possible' (Matthew, 19:26). So, for believers, the quasi-miraculous feat of 'Ali at Khaybar need not be relegated to the realm of fantasy.

Moreover, from an esoteric point of view, what was being demonstrated through 'Ali at Khaybar can be understood in the light of the following Qur'anic verse: 'You [O Prophet] threw not when you threw; rather, it was God who threw' (8:17). This refers to the Prophet's act of throwing pebbles at the Qurayshi army during the Battle of Badr, an act which was understood by all as symbolising the victory of the Muslims. It was understood by the mystically inclined in accordance with the principle of divine power being manifested through the Prophet, a principle referred to directly by the *hadith qudsi* cited earlier, describing the saint, the 'friend' of God: 'When I love him, I become his hearing by which he hears, his sight by which he sees, his hand by which he strikes, and his foot by which he walks.'

'The hand by which he strikes': the hand with which 'Ali wielded the gate as a shield was, in a certain sense, the hand of God, and this by no means makes 'Ali God; it means that 'Ali's degree of proximity to God was such that God manifested something of His knowledge, power and grace through the faculties and even the limbs of His 'friend'. Rumi has 'Ali say, in the *Mathnawi*: 'In war I am (manifesting the truth of) "you did not throw when you threw" (8:17); I am (but) as the sword, and the wielder is the (divine) Sun' (Rumi, *Mathnawi*, 1:3789). 'Ali's superhuman feat at Khaybar, from this point of view, was a sign of divine power, a dramatic proof of God. The fact that 'Ali did not attribute the act to himself might be seen by some as an even more marvellous sign—a sign of his utter humility, his complete self-effacement before God, the sole source of power and grace.

In Islamic spirituality, it is not just amazing feats of strength that are to be attributed to divine grace, but all positive human actions, including all acts of cognition and comprehension, from the sensorial and conventional to the intellectual and spiritual. The Qur'an tells us: 'There is nothing like Him; and He is the Hearer, the Seer' (42:11). God, alone, is the One who hears and sees: our acts of hearing and seeing are but 'metaphorical' (*majazi*) or apparent, while His hearing and seeing is real (*haqiqi*). It is, therefore, God who is the true 'agent' or 'actor' in all of our apparent acts. The 'friend of God' is one who knows this and thereby proclaims, with 'Ali, the statement we just heard through Rumi's inspired poetry: 'I have removed the baggage of self out of the way, I have deemed (what is) other than God to be non-existence.' 'Ali boldly declares, again according to Rumi, that he is indeed the 'lion of God' (*shir-e Haqqam*), not the lion of his own passion (*hawa*): since he has been liberated from his ego, he attributes all glory to God, and for this reason he can claim 'my deed bears witness to my religion' (*Mathnawi*, 1:3788)—that is, not to 'my heroism'. The hero of Khaybar teaches us, therefore, that true heroism is the fruit of absolute faith in God, combined with humility and self-effacement before Him: the ultimate source and sole 'agent' of all power and glory. As we saw in Chapter 1, this chivalric youth, *al-fata*, who was to become the epitome of an entire tradition of Muslim chivalry (*futuwwa*), only once claimed a triumph as his own: when he was fatally struck by the poisoned sword of the assassin, he uttered the words, 'I have triumphed, by the Lord of the Ka'ba!'

♦

In the time of the Prophet, 'Ali distinguished himself not only on the field of battle, but also in reconciliation and peace-making. His resort to warfare was always in self-defence, in line with the Qur'anic principle cited above, and the underlying intention was always to establish peace and justice. In the aftermath of the peaceful conquest of Mecca (8/630), 'Ali successfully resolved a serious crisis precipitated by Khalid b. al-Walid, who had been sent by the Prophet to invite various tribes to embrace Islam peacefully. The tribesmen of Banu Jadhima were promised security by Khalid if they laid down their arms; however, Khalid killed them treacherously once they were disarmed. The Prophet was outraged, and immediately sent 'Ali on a peace mission. The result was a peaceful resolution of the dispute, 'Ali having not just offered compensation for those killed, but also determined the appropriate compensation for other damages suffered by the tribe. He returned to the Prophet, who praised him highly and then repeated three times: 'O God, I am innocent before You of what Khalid has done.'

Another of 'Ali's merits was his being chosen by the Prophet to convey and recite on his behalf a chapter of the Qur'an. In 9/631, he was instructed by the Prophet to recite the opening six verses of the newly revealed Surat al-Bara'a ('The Immunity'; also known as *al-Tawba*, 'Repentance', sura no. 9) to the pilgrims performing the Hajj at Mecca. Abu Bakr had already been sent to lead the pilgrim caravan going to Mecca from Medina. When 'Ali told Abu Bakr that he, 'Ali, was to recite the chapter even though Abu Bakr was leading the pilgrimage, the latter was disconcerted and asked the Prophet, upon his return to Mecca, whether something had been revealed about him that disqualified him from conveying the new revelation to the assembled pilgrims. The Prophet's reply was, 'No, I was commanded that I or someone from the people of my Household should convey it.'

Another example of 'Ali's ability to resolve disputes peacefully and act as an arbitrator and judge, despite his young age, is his mission to Yemen in 10/632. He was sent by the Prophet to engage in debate and dialogue with tribes who were still pagan, and to adjudicate between them in their disputes. It is reported that 'Ali was hesitant at first, due to his lack of experience in this domain. The Prophet is said to have placed his hand on 'Ali's breast and said: 'O God, guide his heart and strengthen his tongue.' Imam 'Ali added, when he recounted this incident later, 'After this, I never doubted in my ability to judge between two men.' He first went to the large and influential tribe of Hamdan, who all entered Islam peacefully, so deeply impressed were they by the justice and wisdom of this extraordinarily radiant young man. When the Prophet was told about this, he made a prophecy that came true: 'After Hamdan's embrace of Islam, the rest of the Yemenis will follow them into the faith.'

Imam 'Ali and the 'People of the Prophet's Household' (Ahl al-Bayt)

Hazrat Fatima and Imam 'Ali are venerated as the forebears of the Prophet's progeny, the *sadat* (singular *sayyid*, literally 'lord'). The Prophet, 'Ali, Fatima, al-Hasan and al-Husayn are referred to in Persian as the *panj tan* ('five bodies'), and they constitute the immediate referent of the term *ahl al-bayt* (people of the [Prophet's] household). The following verse of the Qur'an refers to this group as follows: 'Truly God only wishes to remove all impurity (*al-rijs*) from you, O *Ahl al-Bayt*, and to purify you with utter purification' (33:33). It is asserted in a wide range of sources that after the revelation of this verse the Prophet called for Fatima, 'Ali and their two sons, al-Hasan and al-Husayn, and declared that his Ahl al-Bayt consisted of these four persons, together with himself as the fifth.

For the Shi'is, the divine 'purification' mentioned in the verse implies that Imam 'Ali and the other members of the Ahl al-Bayt are impeccable (*ma'sum*), rendered incapable of committing any sin or major error. The Ahl al-Bayt are also referred to as the *ahl al-kisa'*, 'people of the cloak', because in certain narrations of this event the Prophet is reported to have covered these four persons with his cloak, saying 'This is my Ahl al-Bayt.' This is said to have occurred during the visit to

55

Medina of the Christian delegation from Najran in the eighth
or ninth year of the Hijra.

The importance of the Ahl al-Bayt is expressed in another
verse in which the Prophet is instructed, 'Say: I ask you for
no reward, save love of kinfolk (*qurba*)' (42:23). According to
several of the most influential commentators on the Qur'an,
the referent of 'kinfolk' in this verse is the Prophet's Ahl al-
Bayt. This interpretation is reinforced by the Prophet's saying
'The people of my household [*ahl bayti*], I call God to your
minds in regard to the people of my household,' repeating this
three times according to most narrations, Sunni and Shi'i alike.
Love of the Prophet's family is thus explicitly called for by
the Qur'an, and by the Prophet himself. The extent to which
the Prophet's family are to be revered by all Muslims is also
indicated by the fact that blessings are to be invoked upon
his *al* (the 'a' here is long), or progeny, as a prolongation of
the blessings to be invoked upon him. The Qur'an instructs
the believers: 'Truly, God and His angels bless the Prophet. O
ye who believe, bless him and greet him with peace' (33:56).
When this verse was revealed, the Prophet was asked how
to perform this 'blessing' (the greeting of 'peace' being clear
enough). The Prophet told them to use the following formula,
which has entered all the traditions of devotion in Islam, as
well as figuring as a key ritual incantation in all the mystical
orders:

> 'O God, bless Muhammad and the progeny of Muham-
> mad, as You have blessed Abraham and the progeny of
> Abraham. Truly, You are the Praised, the Glorious...'

The mention of Abraham is significant, as it demonstrates the
universal scope of the Islamic conception of prophethood.
The great importance of this blessing, which is recited during
the canonical prayer in some of the Muslim schools of law,
is stressed in the following lines, taken from a poem by

Imam Shafi'i, founder of one of the four schools of Sunni jurisprudence:

> Loving you, O family of the household of the Prophet
>   of God,
>
> is an obligation [*fard*] from God in the Qur'an which
>   He revealed;
>
> Sufficient to show the grandeur of your dignity
>
> is that one who blesses you not—no prayer has he.

We should repeat here the already mentioned *thaqalayn* saying: 'Truly, I am leaving behind amongst you the two weighty things (*al-thaqalayn*): the Book of God and my Ahl al-Bayt, they will not be parted from each other until they return to me at *al-hawd* [the paradisal pool].' Quite apart from the esoteric implications of this saying, one sees the way in which the teachings of the Qur'an are put into practice by the Prophet's Ahl al-Bayt, and how the actions of the Ahl al-Bayt often served as the 'occasional cause' (*sabab nuzul*) of Qur'anic revelation. One of the most important examples of the latter can be seen in relation to the Surat al-Insan ('The Human Being', no.76), which was said to be revealed after the following episode. Hasan and Husayn were ill, and the Prophet recommended that their parents, 'Ali and Fatima, take a vow to fast for three days if the boys recovered. They did recover, and so the whole family (including their maid, Fidda) fulfilled the vow, fasting for three days, with only some barley-bread and water with which to break their fast at the end of each day. As they were about to break their fast on the first day, a beggar came and asked for food. The family gave away the bread they had prepared, and broke their fast with water alone. On the second day, an orphan did what the beggar had done the previous day. Again, the holy family gave away their bread, breaking their fast only with water. On the third day, it was a prisoner who came to their door asking for food: yet again, the Ahl al-Bayt gave away their bread. Then the Sura was revealed, in which the following verses make specific mention of the selfless charity of the Ahl al-Bayt:

> They [the 'slaves of God'] keep their vow and fear a day
>   whereof the evil is wide-spreading,
>
> And feed with food the needy, the orphan and the
>   prisoner, for love of Him,
>
> [Saying]: 'We feed you, for the sake of God only [lit. 'for
>   the Face of God']. We seek no reward nor thanks
>   from you.'

Among the many important teachings of the Ahl al-Bayt here is that charity must be accomplished in the correct spirit: by an absence of any desire for acknowledgement, reward, or recognition. One is generous to others only 'for the sake of God'—one seeks neither 'reward nor thanks' from those who receive one's help. This spirit ensures that compassion for one's fellow human beings is manifested with a view to the ultimate aim: outward charitable action emerges from, and in turn reinforces, one's inward spiritual aspiration. When gentle compassion and spiritual consciousness come together in this way, moral conscience leads to metaphysical consciousness: one's charitable action clarifies one's spiritual vision, the 'Face of God' is more clearly seen by a heart adorned by the beauty of virtue and enlightened by the remembrance of God. Exemplary morality translates into transformative spirituality. This message is reinforced by verses in the Surat al-Layl ('The Night', 92), relating to the 'most pious' (al-atqa; according to certain commentators, referring to Abu Bakr when he purchased Bilal at a high price to prevent his being tortured by his owners). The 'most pious' person is one who 'gives his wealth in order to purify himself; nobody possesses any good thing which might constitute a reward for this person—for he seeks only the Face of his Lord most High. And he, indeed, will be content' (92:18–21).

A deeper mystical significance of the Ahl al-Bayt is brought out by the commentators who draw attention to their designation in this Sura as 'slaves of God' (*'ibad Allah*), in contradistinction to the 'righteous' (*al-abrar*) at verses 5–6. While 'the righteous' drink from a cup containing drink mixed with the wine of the fountain called Kafur, the slaves of God drink directly from the fountain itself, 'making it gush forth abundantly' (76:5–6). 'Abd al-Razzaq al-Kashani, author of one of the most important esoteric commentaries, describes the Ahl al-Bayt who drink directly from the fountain as follows:

> The slaves are [themselves] the sources of this Fountain; there is no duality or otherness... were it otherwise, it would not be the Fountain of *Kafur*, because of the darkness of the veil of egotism (*ana'iyya*) and duality (Kashani, *Tafsir*, 76:5–6).

The 'slaves' do not belong to themselves, but are wholly possessed by the Lord. But, insofar as they are given existence by the Lord, their identity is one with the very substance—the 'wine'—of Paradise. This wine therefore flows into the world the more these slaves drink from it. Their 'drinking' from this wine, while on earth, can be understood as their remembrance of God, their invocations, meditations, recitations: the long hours each night and day that the Ahl al-Bayt were known to spend in prayer. The wine which gushes forth from Paradise to this world through the Ahl al-Bayt is the light of knowledge, the sweetness of virtue, the inebriating overflow of their remembrance of God. 'Down from me torrents do pour,' said Imam 'Ali, 'up to me no bird can soar.'

♦

The best known *hadith* regarding 'Ali, already discussed in the previous chapter, was uttered by the Prophet after his final pilgrimage to Mecca, in the year 10/632, at a pool midway between Mecca and Medina known as Ghadir Khumm. The

Prophet assembled all the pilgrims, had a pulpit erected and delivered a sermon to the thousands of returning pilgrims. It culminated in the statement: 'For whomever I am the *mawla*, 'Ali is his *mawla*,' and included the supplication: 'O God, befriend the one who befriends him, and be the enemy of whoever opposes him'—a supplication which evokes the *hadith qudsi* discussed in Chapter 1 concerning the 'friend of God': 'I declare war on whoever opposes one of My friends.'

For Shi'is, both the spiritual and the temporal meaning of '*mawla*' are merged in this prophetic declaration, so that the Prophet's naming of 'Ali as *mawla* is understood to be at once an explicit designation (*nass*) of 'Ali as political successor to the Prophet and a public declaration of 'Ali's spiritual authority. For most Sunnis, the statement indicates the special proximity of 'Ali to the Prophet, and for many mystically inclined Sunnis it goes further, showing that, after the Prophet, 'Ali was the spiritual master and mystical guide of the Muslim community, as manifested by his being the forebear of all Sufi orders. The most common Sunni position is that the Ghadir Khumm declaration did not imply that 'Ali was to be the Prophet's successor in the political domain. Nonetheless, the description of 'Ali as the *mawla* of all Muslims remains of the greatest significance in spiritual terms. 'Umar is reported to have come and said to 'Ali, 'Congratulations, you have become my *mawla* and the *mawla* of every Muslim.' So, although the Ghadir Khumm declaration has been the subject of heated dispute through the ages, it has also been of immense importance in heightening the receptivity of countless Muslims of all persuasions to the spiritual mystery of sainthood, the *walaya*, embodied by 'Ali.

It is necessary to discuss briefly the notion of *Shi'at 'Ali*, the 'supporters (or followers or partisans) of 'Ali'. The term itself, *Shi'at 'Ali*, appears to have first been coined by the Prophet himself. Even during the Prophet's lifetime, a small group was already known for their particular love for 'Ali. According to

Shi'i and Sunni sources alike, it is to this group of companions that the Prophet referred in his answer to a question about the Qur'anic verse 98:7: 'Those who have faith and do righteous deeds—they are the best of created beings' (*khayr al-bariyya*). Tabari, among others, refers to the report that the Prophet recited this verse and then said to 'Ali: 'You, O 'Ali and your *shi'a*' (Tabari, *Jami'*, 30:320). Similarly, in his comment on 98:7, the later Sunni authority and Qur'an commentator, Jalal al-Din al-Suyuti (d. 1505) refers to the report that the Prophet recited this verse and then addressed 'Ali: 'That is, you and your *shi'a*, on the Day of Judgement, pleased and well-pleasing' (Suyuti, *Durr*, 6:379). According to the companion, Jabir b. 'Abd Allah, the Prophet, upon seeing 'Ali, said, 'By Him in whose hand is my soul, truly he and his Shi'a are triumphant on the Day of Judgement,' after which 98:7 was revealed. The narration continues: 'So the companions of the Prophet used to say, when meeting 'Ali, "the best of created beings (*khayr al-bariyya*) has come"' (Ibn Mardawayh, 347).

The members of this group of companions who were known for their particular devotion to the person of 'Ali were Salman al-Farisi, Abu Dharr al-Ghifari, 'Ammar b. Yasir and Miqdad b. Amr. As Husain Jafri notes: 'Historically it cannot be denied... that these men formed the nucleus of the first Alid party, or the Shi'a' (Jafri, 53). These four persons are therefore regarded by later Shi'a tradition as 'the four pillars' of Shi'ism. At the historical origin and the spiritual heart of Shi'ism, then, is the notion of fidelity to 'Ali, and through him to the spiritual principle that he personified, *walaya*. In this context, *walaya* denotes two complementary principles, the first being spiritual authority or guardianship, deriving from proximity to God, love, intimacy or friendship with Him, as noted above; and the second being fidelity, devotion, affiliation manifested by the follower toward the one qualified by *walaya*, the *wali Allah*, 'friend of God'.

It is important to repeat what we have said earlier: neither personal devotion to ʿAli, nor the spiritual orientation towards the *walaya* he is deemed to embody, is confined to Shiʿa Islam; it extends to all the schools of Islam, for veneration of ʿAli as head of the Ahl al-Bayt ('People of the Household') of the Prophet is found throughout the length and breadth of the Muslim world, from the inception of Islam to the present. A fine example is the poem in which al-Shafiʿi, founder of one of the four schools of Sunni jurisprudence, claims to have befriended 'the best imam, the best guide (*khayra imam wa khayra hadi*)' (al-Shafiʿi, 27; see also Jaʿfariyan, *Tarikh-i tashayyuʿ*), this supreme love for ʿAli, needless to say, going hand in hand with the highest respect for the first three caliphs.

Indeed, the Prophet's designation of the Shiʿa of ʿAli can be interpreted, in accordance with our discussion of the universal nature of the *ʿAlawi* archetype in Chapter 1, in a supra-confessional sense, to include all those souls—of whatever religion—who orient themselves or affiliate themselves to the principle of *walaya*, loving the person or persons in their religion who are themselves personifications of *walaya*, and thus make manifest through their very being the celestial fruit of the spiritual quest.

As noted in the introduction, the acrimonious debates over Imam ʿAli in later theological and ideological contexts are overshadowed by his unifying role in the spiritual and mystical traditions of Islam. One of the most important figures in this regard is Sayyid Haydar Amuli (d. 1385), whose writings can be seen as building a bridge between Sunni Sufism and Shiʿa spirituality, or *ʿirfan*. He asserts that despite the formal, juridical differences between Sunni and Shiʿa, when it comes to spirituality, the terms Sufi and Shiʿi are different names of one and the same orientation toward ultimate reality (*haqiqa*), the inner dimension of Islam. Here, ʿAli is seen as an ideal personification of this *haqiqa* and, after the Prophet, the chief spiritual guide leading mystical aspirants along the path to the *haqiqa*. It is for this reason that Amuli says that if one needed to find, among the sayings of the saints, means by which the *haqiqa* of *tawhid* can be disclosed, the sayings of 'Ali suffice, for he is 'the most tremendous among them and the most complete among them' (Amuli, *Jami'*, 301).

As noted earlier, Ibn 'Arabi maintains that 'Ali was the closest of all human spirits to the Prophet in the primordial 'cloud' which foreshadowed all manifested creation, referring to 'Ali as 'imam of the world and secret of all the prophets.' This view of 'Ali's *walaya* is close to that found within Shi'a sources. For example, as regards the proximity between the Prophet and Imam 'Ali in the spiritual realm prior to the creation of the world, we find the Prophet addressing 'Ali thus: 'O 'Ali, God was and nothing was with Him, whereupon He created me and created you as two spirits from the light of His majesty... you and I are of a single light and a single clay.' Similarly, as regards 'Ali constituting the 'secret' of all the prophets: 'The *walaya* of Ali is inscribed in all the books of the prophets; every other messenger was only sent to proclaim the prophethood of Muhammad and the *walaya* of Ali' (al-Saffar, *Basa'ir*, 72).

The principle of *walaya* is so tightly woven into the fabric of spiritual realization in Shi'a Islam that the Shi'a refer to themselves frequently as 'the people of *walaya*' (*ahl al-walaya*; Amir-Moezzi, *Spirituality*, 231). The *ahl al-walaya* are thus identical to the *Shi'at 'Ali*, and this leads us to pose the question: how could there have arisen a group of the Prophet's companions who manifested such a degree of veneration for 'Ali that they could be designated as his *Shi'a*, a designation legitimated and ratified by the Prophet himself? Answering this question helps us to appreciate the spirit motivating Shi'a Muslims, and to dispel various misconceptions, such as the absurd notion that the Shi'a are more devoted to 'Ali and the imams than to the Prophet. What is clear about this early group of supporters of 'Ali is that they did not in any way consider their devotion to him as a distraction from, or dilution of, their devotion to the Prophet. Rather, their devotion to 'Ali can be seen as an overflow of their devotion to the Prophet, and served only to bring them closer to his spiritual presence.

A conventional theological answer to the question why such a group of followers of 'Ali should have formed in the lifetime of the Prophet is this: the Shi'a of 'Ali recognised his authority as an imam, a spiritual leader, possessing an authority bestowed upon him by God and the Prophet. But a more nuanced answer emerges as a result of what 'Ali b. al-Husayn (the fourth Shi'i imam) said, implicitly, about the difference of degrees of spiritual knowledge within the very group of his close companions: 'If Abu Dharr knew what was in the heart of Salman, he would have killed him' (cited in Amir-Moezzi, *Spirituality*, 294). Whereas Abu Dharr's devotion to 'Ali was based upon fundamentally exoteric notions of faith, Salman's was fed by an intuition of the esoteric mysteries which were not only disclosed by 'Ali to him, but also rendered spiritually accessible and thus realizable by him. Those who 'had ears to hear,' those who could 'read between the lines' of the many allusions to the esoteric depths of the faith made by 'Ali, responded to his teachings and his presence according to the depth of their own intuition of the mysteries alluded to in those teachings. It was thanks to his depth of understanding that Salman was referred to by 'Ali (and, according to some sources, by the Prophet) as being 'one of us, the Ahl al-Bayt' (see Corbin *En Islam*, 1:264ff., for a profound discussion of the implications of this 'adoption' of Salman into the prophetic household).

However, both Salman and Abu Dharr, representing archetypes along a spectrum of devotion ranging from the most formal and outward (*zahir*) dimensions to the most subtle and inward (*batin*), would have appreciated their devotion to 'Ali as deriving from, and therefore subordinated to, their devotion to the Prophet. As noted earlier, it was the

Prophet himself who fostered, cultivated and clearly approved of this devotion to 'Ali, knowing that it served only to enhance devotion to the Prophet, to Islam, to God; and to deepen receptivity to the inner, sanctifying graces transmitted by God through the Prophet's *nubuwwa*.

Let us return to the key prophetic saying referring to Ali's *walaya*, the Ghadir Khumm declaration. In some versions of the tradition, the Prophet makes this declaration after first asking the congregation: 'Am I not closer (*awla*) to the believers than their own selves?' This is understood as an evocation of the following Qur'anic verse: 'The Prophet is closer to the believers than their selves, and his wives are [as] their mothers. And the owners of kinship are closer to one another in the ordinance of God than [other] believers and emigrants...' (33:6). All Shi'a, and some Sunni, sources have mentioned the relevance of this verse to the Ghadir declaration, as the verse was revealed just prior to it: 'O Messenger! Convey that which has been revealed unto you from your Lord. If you do it not, you would not have conveyed His Message. And God will defend you against the people' (Q 5:67). Similarly, great stress is placed by the Shi'a on the fact that Q 5:3 was revealed during the Hajj, that is, just a matter of days before Ghadir. The key part of this verse reads as follows: 'This day I have perfected for you your religion, and completed my favour upon you, and have chosen for you *islam* as religion.' The conveying of the Message in all its completeness mentioned in 5:67 is explicitly identified with the Ghadir declaration of Ali's *walaya*; and the latter, in turn, is identified by Shi'a theologians with the 'perfection' and 'completion' of the religion of Islam (see Amir-Moezzi, *Spirituality*, 237–239). This assertion is underlined by the fact that in one version of the sermon given by the Prophet at Ghadir there is the famous saying: 'I leave behind me two weighty things (*thaqalayn*): the Book of God and my Ahl al-Bayt.'

The 'Bequest' of the Prophet

The Prophet died on 13 Rabi' al-Awwal 11/8 June 632. It is reported that, before passing away, he was seen to whisper something to 'Ali. When asked afterwards what the Prophet had said, 'Ali replied: 'He taught me of a thousand gates of knowledge, and each gate opened for me another thousand gates. He made a bequest to me which I will undertake, if God wishes' (Mufid, *Irshad*, 132). This is an extremely important statement for many reasons, one of which, on the historical plane, is that the Prophet did not leave a formal, public, written will. The fact that Imam 'Ali did not reveal the details of the 'bequest' is significant, for it can be seen as yet another example of an *ishara*, or allusion, in relation to 'Ali's *walaya*. The esoteric or hidden nature of the bequest is made all the more mysterious by being linked to 'a thousand gates of knowledge,' each of which opened another thousand gates, all within a few seconds of a whispered teaching. We are in the presence, then, of a 'million' sciences, which can be understood as a symbol for the intrinsically innumerable; or as an allusion to a mode of knowledge that is qualitative rather than quantitative, principial and universal rather than phenomenal and particular. That is, it refers to a metaphysical, supra-rational mode of cognition which, opening out on to the universal Truth, comprises the essence of all possible particular truths, symbolised by a million gates of knowledge. The knowledge in question is thus the fruit of a mystical state of consciousness; it is as if the Prophet wished to share with Imam 'Ali a spiritual 'taste' (*dhawq*) of the Infinite, thereby attuning his heart to the quintessence of prophetic knowledge, which is, ultimately, knowledge of God. It is as if the Prophet's deathbed transmission of a mode of spiritual consciousness enabled Imam 'Ali to perceive with even greater depth the mystery of the inescapable presence of God, whose 'Face', as the Qur'an states, is there wherever we turn (Q 2:115); and to perfect Imam 'Ali's knowledge of the relationship between the non-manifest or 'hidden' world (*'alam al-ghayb*) and the manifest world (*'alam al-shahada*): that scarcely imaginable interface between the two realms of Being, an interface determined by the divine 'measure' (*qadar*) of the destiny of all beings in the cosmos.

It is as if, through this allusive teaching, the Prophet wished to give Imam 'Ali an opening to the divine 'measure' of all things, to see things as God sees them (*sub specie aeternitatis*: 'from the point of view of eternity'); to see phenomena in the light of their principles; to give him an insight into the unimaginably complex intertwining networks of beings and events in the matrix of the cosmos; and to see something of the way in which this fabric of the cosmos is woven by the divine measure and decree (*al-qadar wa'l-qada*) in accordance with the divine knowledge. These two qualities of God, *al-Qadir*, 'He who determines all things' and *al-'Alim*, 'The Knower', are implied in the following verse of the Qur'an, cited earlier, in which the celestial potentialities—from which all manifested things flow down to earth—are referred to as 'treasuries': 'There is no thing but that its treasuries are with Us; and We only send it down in a known measure (*qadar ma'lum*)' (15:21). For God, all things, past, present and future are determined and known (thus, 'measured') in the eternal 'now'. Therefore, through revelation, to the prophets, and through inspiration, to the saints, certain events in the future can be rendered visible to the 'eye' of the heart. As we shall see in the following chapter, Imam 'Ali speaks of souls yet to be born, who were nonetheless 'witnessing' his victory at the Battle of Jamal.

Applying the logic of the above considerations, we may be assisted in our effort to speculate about the content of this final teaching of the Prophet if we bear in mind another prophetic teaching given by the Prophet during his last days. He was seen to whisper in the ear of his daughter, Fatima. She wept. Then he whispered something else, and she smiled.

She explained afterwards: when the Prophet told her he would die from his illness, she wept; and then, when he told her that she would be the first to join him in Paradise, she smiled (Mufid, *Irshad*, 133). It is possible, therefore, that one of the 'gates' of knowledge opened by the Prophet to Imam 'Ali was a prophecy about his own death: that 'Ali would die a martyr, but that his killer would be someone who called himself a Muslim. And that both of his sons (the Prophet's grandsons, Hasan and Husayn) would also die as martyrs, also treacherously killed by individuals who called themselves Muslims. For someone of the spiritual wisdom of Imam 'Ali, such a prophecy would indeed have opened thousands of gates of knowledge. It would have spoken volumes, both on the plane of this world—the innumerable causal chains of phenomena leading to such unbelievably absurd outcomes; and on the plane of principles, moral, and intellectual, spiritual and divine, in terms of which the divine will is seen, by the eye of the heart, as the ultimate source of all events, all phenomena, all things without exception. Past and future would be collapsed and viewed as a single instant from the viewpoint of eternity. Or: past history and future destiny would be intertwined within one and the same mystery: a mystery woven out of the unfathomable will, the infinite wisdom, and the unimpeachable goodness of God.

Taking further this line of speculation, the specific 'bequest' of the Prophet to 'Ali may have been something like this: after my death, be prepared for gross injustices and awful absurdities that will befall you, and after you, to our family, the Ahl al-Bayt; respond to these injustices and absurdities with total resignation (*islam*) to the will of God, together with patience, contentment and trust: do this, and you will be granted perfect inner peace. You will be 'saved', in other words, from falling victim to despair, distress and anxiety, however awful be the ordeals through which you have to pass. This is closely related to a well-known saying of the Prophet, in which he compared his Ahl al-Bayt to Noah's Ark: whoever enters it will be saved, and whoever abandons it will perish (we shall return to this saying in Chapter 4).

If this is remotely close to what was in fact imparted, it would be a commentary upon the well known prophetic teaching: 'There is no strength or power save through God': that is, nothing happens but by the will of God. In the words of another saying of similar import: 'That which God wills shall come to pass, and that which He does not will, shall not come to pass.' This apparent truism expresses a profoundly empowering teaching, helping the believer to accept absolutely everything that happens as the will of God, however incomprehensible be the injustices on the plane of ordinary logic, however awful be the trials for the soul. Such acceptance of the will of God does not preclude struggling against the injustices, and making every effort to surmount the trials; it simply means that one accepts, in advance, whatever outcome God has pre-eternally ordained for every single event that actually comes to pass; one accepts, in other words, the possibility that the trials and the injustices may only be overcome in the Hereafter. One accepts the trial as a means by which one's faith and patience is proved. Then, it is possible that God will bestow a higher station upon the soul: the capacity to remain in inner peace and imperturbable contentment, even in the very midst of the earthly tribulation. For, however severe be the outward trials of this world, faith in God will grant the believer inner serenity, since 'the faithful are well in all circumstances.' It is all a question of how deep the faith of the believer is, the degree to which faith inspires the heart, rather than residing simply as a concept in the mind.

◆

There is another aspect of this discourse to consider, that of mystical initiation, the transmission of a theurgic energy, or an initiatic power, the opening of a 'gate' to the ultimate metaphysical realisation. First, let us recall the saying of the Prophet: 'I am the city of knowledge, and 'Ali is its gate' (*bab*). In this light, the opening of a thousand gates, each opening a further thousand, might be seen as the outward differentiation of what is implicit in the single gate referred to by the Prophet, the gate leading to prophetic consciousness in all its plenitude. According to Amir-Moezzi, the formula of one thousand gates or teachings, each of which opens or leads to a further thousand, denotes mystical initiation in the Shi'i context (Amir-Moezzi, *Divine Guide*, 121). Secondly, there are several other versions of this transmission from the Prophet to the Imam according to which the Prophet was perspiring profusely while imparting the knowledge, and Imam 'Ali was likewise perspiring while receiving the knowledge (see, for example, al-Saffar, *Basa'ir*, 333–334). Why is this so significant? Because, as is well known in the traditional accounts of the experience of the Prophet while receiving Revelation, he perspired—even in winter, according to several traditions. It is also said that the Prophet's sweat had a fragrance more delightful than musk; and that the beads of sweat on his forehead were like pearls. The Arabic word for 'sweat' (*'araq*) is full of significance. *'Aruq*, from the same root, describes one of noble birth. The poet Imru'l-Qays refers to Adam as *'irq al-thara*, the root of mankind, which evokes the idea of Adam being like the sweat that arises out of the earth when subjected to the creative energy of God. One speaks of the 'sweat of friendship' (*'araq al-khilal*), that which is given to a friend out of love. In its verbal forms, it also signifies the instilling of good disposition. The word for mother-of-pearl (nacre, the material from which natural pearls are formed, layer by layer) is *'irq al-lu'lu'*, 'the root/origin of the pearl' which, again, evokes the idea of the sweat arising out of the substance in the shell, from which the pearl is formed. This leads to certain interesting cosmological doctrines.

In an extraordinary vision of the origin of the cosmos, Ibn

'Arabi sees the 'water of the Throne', from which the cosmos emerges, as a pearl formed by the sweat of the Muhammadan Reality, the sweat itself being the result of a revealing discourse from God to the Prophet in this, his pre-personal, metaphysical Reality. 'I was a Prophet,' he said, 'when Adam was still between water and clay.' According to another saying, the first created entity was a white pearl (identifiable with the Muhammadan Reality, or the Muhammadan Light) which turned to liquid through awe (see Elmore, *Islamic Sainthood*, 391ff., for discussion). In this final discourse of the Prophet to 'Ali, then, might we see something analogous taking place: the transmission of *walaya*, the quintessence of prophetic gnosis, symbolically and 'cosmically' reflecting the primordial act of divine creativity? Initiation into the heart of prophetic revelation participating in the fulgurating power of creative manifestation?

3

Imam 'Ali and the Caliphate

The Principle of *Zuhd*

'Do you think the caliphate adorned 'Ali? No, rather, it was 'Ali who adorned the caliphate.' This famous saying of Ahmad ibn Hanbal, founder of one of the four Sunni schools of law, puts into perspective the relationship between Imam 'Ali and the caliphate. It highlights the distinction between the spiritual values embodied by 'Ali and the worldly contingencies of political life. What made 'Ali the man he was had little to do with politics, even if, as caliph, his wisdom and justice inaugurated a dramatic reform of state policies which, if carried through, would have transformed the moral fibre of Muslim society. Even if those policies were short-lived, the effects of his spiritual vision continue to be felt, reverberating down through the centuries, to our own times.

His influence on the world, however, is to be seen as one of the consequences of his detachment from it. In other words, it was precisely on account of his detachment from the world—his *zuhd*—that he was able to rule with dispassionate justice. If we wish to understand Imam 'Ali's fundamental attitude towards the question of political rule, then we need to understand properly his repeated and insistent emphasis upon *zuhd*.

Imam 'Ali's sayings, sermons and letters are replete with expressions of *zuhd*, a fundamental element of spirituality, which is central to the prophetic teachings and is a key aspect of the prophetic *sunna*, or conduct. The Prophet lived a life of austere simplicity, praying long hours each night, fasting at least twice a week (in addition to the fast of Ramadan), and possessing next to nothing in the way of worldly goods. The Prophet's *zuhd* is summed up in this saying: 'Be in this world as if you were a stranger or a wayfarer.'

Probably speaking about the renowned ascetic Abu Dharr al-Ghifari, Imam 'Ali said in a sermon: 'I once had a brother in God. What made him immense in my eyes was the smallness of the world in his eyes.' 'By God,' he exclaims in another sermon, 'this world of yours is more contemptible in my eyes than a bone of a pig in the hand of a leper.' He compares the world to a snake: 'whose touch is smooth, whose venom is lethal' (*layyin massuha, qatil sammuha*). He makes a similar point in another sermon, while explaining why he accepted the responsibility of the caliphate: 'Had God not taken from the learned [a promise] that they would not acquiesce in the rapacity of the tyrant nor in the hunger of the oppressed... I would truly have flung its reins [that of the caliphate] back upon its withers... and you would indeed have discovered that this world of yours is as insignificant to me as that which drips from the nose of a goat.'

How do we reconcile this fierce renunciation of the world with the fact that 'wherever you turn there is the Face of God' (Q 2:115)?; or with the statement, cited earlier, 'Our Lord, You have not created all this [the cosmos] in vain' (Q 3:191)? Is this degree of *zuhd* not a negation of the beauties of God's creation? Not at all. For *zuhd* is a negation of the world only insofar as the world is seen in its aspect of limitation and transience. It is thus a detachment from the impermanence of the world arising out of an attachment to the eternity of God. Consequently, it goes hand in hand with a love of everything in this world which reflects, albeit fleetingly, the qualities of God. It is therefore not surprising that Imam 'Ali is also capable of devoting entire sermons to the glory and beauty of God's creation (see his famous sermon in the *Nahj* on the peacock, for example). Such beauties are foretastes of the Paradise that the blessed will experience in the Hereafter, and which the heart of Imam 'Ali's consciousness already inhabits in this world.

In a famous saying in the *Nahj*, he chides someone who was excessive in his denunciation of the world, reminding him that 'the world is the place for prostration (*masjid*) of the lovers of God, the place of prayer (*musalla*) of the angels of God, the place of descent for the Revelation of God, and the place of trading (*matjar*) for the friends of God (*awliya' Allah*).' He explains the nature of the 'trading' that takes place for the 'friends of God': their 'earnings' in the world consist of divine mercy (*rahma*), and the 'profit' they gain from the world is Paradise. As he says elsewhere, 'This world is transient, while the Hereafter is permanent; so take [what will be of benefit for you] from the place through which you are temporarily passing for the place where you will permanently abide' (*fakhudhu min mamarrikum li-maqarrikum*).

This fleeting world is meaningful for the Imam only insofar as it prepares us for our permanent home in the Hereafter. But, perhaps paradoxically, what this implies is that this world is of immense significance: it is a stepping stone to Heaven. If one lives well in this world, guided by the Truth, always striving for virtue, avoiding the pitfalls of worldliness and egotism, then this world becomes the threshold of Paradise. Thus, the world itself becomes 'paradisal': it gives us a foretaste of the beatitude to which it leads. As noted earlier, the Imam teaches us that these 'first fruits' of Paradise are 'tasted' by the heart through the happiness produced by beauty, 'inward and outward': on the one hand, beauty of soul, good character, noble intentions; and on the other, the beauty of God's 'signs' in the world. 'We shall show them Our signs on the horizons and in their souls,' the Qur'an tells us (41:53).

Nonetheless, one might baulk at the severity of the Imam's denunciation of the world, shrinking from the rhetorical excess of the images he uses: one might ask, is it really necessary to compare the world to a decaying carcass and a pig's bone? To answer this question, we need to appreciate the particular historical moment at which he acceded to the caliphate. He was attempting nothing less than a total elimination of the gross corruption that had taken root in the political, social and economic structures of Muslim society. This was a society being engulfed by waves of worldliness, greed and materialism, and in which those who had stood against the tide (such as, most prominently, Abu Dharr al-Ghifari, a leading companion of the Prophet) were marginalised and humiliated. The caliphate of his predecessor, 'Uthman, had become fatally undermined precisely by the insatiable hunger for personal wealth, worldly power and self-aggrandisement that drove the political elite into blatant and shameless corruption. It was this corruption that provoked widespread discontent and to revolts that led eventually to the murder of the caliph. After acceding to the caliphate himself, the Imam was thus compelled not only to initiate major new policies to rectify the situation, but also to use his eloquence and imaginative rhetoric to transform attitudes, to warn of the corrupting poison of worldliness, even if this meant going so far in the opposite direction as to appear to denigrate the world.

The Imam's aim in public sermons that castigated 'the world' was, however, not just to preach to the wealthy elites who had accumulated unbelievably massive piles of gold and silver, as if they had become bankers; he also wanted to ensure that ordinary people did not become infected with the virus of worldliness that was rife in society. For many years, the masses had been witness to an ever-rising tide of worldliness, their governors behaving as if all that mattered was material wealth and political power. He felt compelled to rouse the

Muslims out of any passive acceptance of the values inherent in this gross materialism, and to denounce the world in the most striking terms possible. For the Imam, one has the right to enjoy the blessings offered by this world, in due measure; but one also has the duty to be detached from the world, this inner detachment constituting *zuhd*: 'He who knows the world detaches himself (*tazahhad*) from it.' By contrast, someone who knows with certainty that Paradise is his true home cannot but be totally attached to it, constantly inspired by it, and inwardly transformed by it:

> If you were to cast the eye of your heart towards what is described for you of the Garden, your soul would become averse to the adornments of this world—its passions, its pleasures and its embellished scenery. And your soul would be rapt in contemplation of the swaying trees whose roots lie hidden in dunes of musk on the banks of the rivers of the Garden, and the clusters of dazzling pearls hanging down from the branches of its trees.

It would be quite mistaken, therefore, to begin a discussion of the Imam's caliphate as if it were merely a question of 'political' analysis, and as if we can now put aside all 'spiritual' considerations. For we are not dealing with an ordinary person, immersed in, and determined by, the political domain. According to all the sources, the Imam agreed to be caliph with great reluctance, doing so in order to try to re-establish justice, and despite the fact that he deemed the world and all it contains as no more significant than 'what drips from the nose of a goat.' When, immediately after the killing of 'Uthman, crowds came to him proclaiming him caliph, he said it was not for them to decide. He said that only a counsel composed of the veterans of the Battle of Badr—the Muslims with the greatest honour—had the power to appoint the caliph. When these veterans made known their decision, insisting that nobody but 'Ali could be caliph, he still made every effort to avoid becoming the caliph, telling them to appoint a caliph from among themselves, and that he, 'Ali, would prefer to be a minister (*wazir*) rather than the leader (*amir*). But such was the pressure, both from the populace at large and the veterans of Badr, that he finally accepted the position of caliph (Ja'farian, *History*, 200).

It cannot be over-emphasised: what concerned the Imam, first and foremost, was the performance of his duty as an *imam*, that is, as a spiritual guide and religious teacher. He was also perfectly aware of the principle taught by the Prophet: the very desire to rule disqualifies one from ruling. He assumed power as a regrettable necessity, one which was totally subordinate to his principal spiritual duty; political power was seen by the Imam as a means to an end, that end being justice on all levels: social and political, ethical and intellectual, religious and spiritual. 'I bear witness,' he said, 'that God is Justice (*'adl*), and that He acts justly.' Imam 'Ali defined justice as 'putting each thing in its proper place' (a definition identical to that of Plato in the *Republic*). For the Imam, the first 'thing' to be put into its proper place is one's relationship with God; everything else is secondary, and finds its value only in terms of this fundamental relationship. 'Whoso makes sound what is between himself and God,' he says, 'God makes sound what is between him and mankind.' What was paramount for the Imam was helping people to 'make sound' their relationship with God. In his view, justice in society—a pattern of sound and wholesome relationships within and between all classes of society—would inevitably be established, by God's grace, if each member of society had a sound relationship with God. Teaching people how to be true to God was his main concern, whether he was governing the Muslim empire or farming his estate at Yanbu as a private individual.

'Ali and His Predecessors
in the Caliphate

Before looking at the Imam's caliphate, let us look briefly at his relationship with the first three caliphs—Abu Bakr, 'Umar and 'Uthman. The historical evidence is indisputable: he made his oath of allegiance (*ba'ya*) to each caliph in turn. Despite having certain disagreements with them over particular policies and decisions, he followed up his public, formal oath of allegiance, implying recognition of their legitimacy, with constant support, advice and guidance, from which all three benefited greatly.

On the whole, Sunni traditionalists and historians tend to overlook or minimise the disagreements between 'Ali and the first three caliphs, and to downplay 'Ali's claims to be the rightful successor to the Prophet, or deny the authenticity of the reports in which these claims are made. This tendency is motivated by a desire to uphold and consolidate the orthodox position on the first four caliphs, Abu Bakr, 'Umar, 'Uthman and 'Ali: they are 'the rightly-guided caliphs' (*al-khulafa' al-rashidun*), and thus, almost by definition, acted in harmony with each other.

According to this view, despite minor differences of opinion, 'Ali is seen as strongly supporting the rule of the first three caliphs, and acting as trusted and valued counsellor to each of them in turn. Shi'i sources, by contrast, assert that the Prophet's designation (*nass*) of 'Ali as his successor was ignored by the first three caliphs and their supporters, preferring to act according to what they thought best for the community following the death of the Prophet. What is indisputable is that 'Ali adopted a politically quiescent attitude to the rule of his predecessors in the caliphate, acting as a constant source of advice and guidance when he was consulted, but playing no active role in the state apparatus. He assumed a more prominent public role only towards the end of the rule of 'Uthman,

when he attempted to mediate between the rebels and the caliph, and to help the latter redress the widespread grievances
among the populace which led to the rebellion against his rule,
and to his being killed by a group of the rebels besieging his
palace.

Some historical sources, including several sermons in the
Nahj al-balagha, indicate that 'Ali was convinced that he was the
person best qualified to lead the Muslims as caliph. But 'Ali did
not base his claims on the Ghadir Khumm *hadith*, or any other
sayings of the Prophet. Rather, he only invoked the authority
of the Ghadir declaration when he was already caliph, over two
decades after the pledge of Saqifa. Nonetheless, there is little
room for doubt as regards 'Ali's fundamental attitude towards
his own intrinsic right to rule. In many sermons and letters
recorded in the *Nahj al-balagha* and elsewhere, he emphatically
reiterates the pivotal role of the Prophet's Ahl al-Bayt for
the religion of Islam in general; he continuously stresses the
importance of his own role as the leader of the Ahl al-Bayt, and
his duty to lead the Muslim community in particular. It is as if
he were saying that, in an ideal world, spiritual authority and
temporal power should in principle be united; but this world
is far from ideal. If he, as the spiritual authority, does not have
political power, it is his duty to guide and advise those holding
political power to the best of his ability—and this is precisely
what he did.

Let us consider briefly the famous sermon entitled *al-
Shiqshiqiyya*. The sermon gives us the impression that 'Ali
saw himself as the exasperated victim of gross injustice, his
predecessors in the caliphate being depicted as usurpers of his
right to rule. However, we must note that its authenticity has
been the subject of dispute. If our aim is to build bridges of
understanding, and not to score confessional points, we would
do well to consider the view on this sermon expressed by
Ibn Maytham al-Bahrani, Shi'i author of the most important
philosophical commentary on the *Nahj*: 'One group among

the Shiʻis claim the sermon... has the highest degree of authenticity (*tawatur*), being transmitted by multiple chains of narrators,' he writes, 'while a group among the Sunnis deny this, going so far as to say: "No complaint about the caliphate has been expressed by Ali." They attribute the sermon to Al-Radi' (Ibn Maytham, *Sharh*, 1:251).

For his own part, Ibn Maytham claims that both groups have gone beyond the bounds of moderation, the Shiʻis being guilty of 'exaggeration' (*ifrat*), the Sunnis, of 'negligence' (*tafrit*). As regards the Shiʻi position, he writes that the most renowned Shiʻi scholars do not make the claim of *tawatur* for the sermon. He accepts the fact that 'Ali did indeed have grievances, and that this fact is conveyed by so many sources as to be undeniable. But this does not bestow the status of *tawatur* on the sermon as a whole. In other words, it is not necessary to believe that every word of this sermon was uttered by 'Ali. This is very important, for such a position makes it easier for Shiʻis to uphold the rights of 'Ali to the caliphate without having to denigrate the rule of the first three caliphs, still less to call them 'usurpers'. We would then propose the following: since 'Ali was able to recognise the legitimacy of the rule of each of the three caliphs in turn, despite his belief in his superior right to the caliphate, then Shiʻis may well follow his example, by believing in his superior right to rule, on the one hand, while respecting the legitimacy of the rule of Abu Bakr, 'Umar and 'Uthman, on the other.

The following incident reinforces this point of view. A poem was composed against those deemed to have deprived 'Ali of his rights:

> I never believed that the leadership of the Umma would
>   be denied to the clan of Banu Hashim, or from
>   Imam Abu al-Hasan [i.e., 'Ali].
>
> Was not 'Ali the first person to pray in the direction of
>   your *qibla*?

Is he not the most knowledgeable among you regarding
the Qur'an and the Messenger's Sunna?

Was he not the nearest person to the Prophet? Did
Gabriel not assist him in preparing the body of the
Prophet for burial?

When 'Ali was informed about this poem and others of its
ilk, he dispatched a messenger telling the local governor to
order the cessation of this kind of composition and recitation,
saying: 'The welfare of religion is more lovable to us than
anything else' (Ibn Abi'l-Hadid, *Sharh*, 6:21).

Madelung sums up an important argument made by the
Shi'is: 'In the Qur'an, the descendants and close kin of the
prophets are their heirs also in respect to kingship (*mulk*),
rule (*hukm*), wisdom (*hikma*), the book and the imamate'
(Madelung, *Succession*, 17). If the prophets mentioned in the
Qur'an were succeeded by their near of kin in spiritual
and political terms, the argument runs, it is evident that
Muhammad should be succeeded by his.

'Ali's pledge of allegiance to Abu Bakr, and to his two
successors, is taken by Sunni scholars as evidence of 'Ali's
acceptance of the legitimacy of the caliphate as established by
his three predecessors. By contrast, Shi'i scholars downplay
the significance of 'Ali's *bay'a*, arguing that it was done out
of political expediency, motivated by a desire to preserve the
unity of the Umma. Certain Shi'is refer to controversial early
reports such as those found in a work entitled *Kitab Sulaym b.
Qays* (a work deemed by majoritarian Shi'i scholars to fall into
the category of 'extremism,' *ghuluww*); and argue on their basis
that the *bay'a* of 'Ali was either the result of coercion, or that
he was only engaging in *taqiyya*—'protective dissimulation'. In
other words, that he proffered the oath of allegiance only out
of a desire to save his life. Such a view, however, seems to us
to be devoid of credibility, given that 'Ali was not the kind
of person—to put it mildly—who could be forced by anyone
to do anything that contradicted his conviction of what was

right, or that contravened a clear mandate given him by the Prophet. One only has to think of his son, al-Husayn, to see the impossibility of a member of the Ahl al-Bayt taking an oath of allegiance to an illegitimate ruler. As the Sufi master Khwaja Muʿin al-Din Chishti said in a Persian poem famous throughout the Indian subcontinent: 'Husayn gave his head, but not his hand, to Yazid.' Like son, like father: no right was superior to that of the truth—there is no room for *taqiyya* when it comes to making a formal, public oath of allegiance to a ruler.

ʿAli's Oath of Allegiance

It is possible to argue that ʿAli's *bayʿa* to Abu Bakr was made for the sake of Muslim unity, and that it was at the same time an expression of ʿAli's recognition of the political legitimacy of Abu Bakr's rule, a legitimacy based on Abu Bakr's personal qualities of piety and sincerity, his adherence to Islamic principles, and his intention to govern the Muslim community with justice, equity and propriety. Against the background of Abu Bakr's sincere service to the Prophet and the cause of Islam from the very beginning of the Prophet's call, the following two pieces of evidence might be cited in support of this argument. First, in a well-attested report, Abu Sufyan came to ʿAli after the pledge had been made to Abu Bakr, inciting ʿAli to rise up and fight for his rights, offering to 'fill the streets of Medina with soldiers and cavalry' on his behalf. ʿAli rejected this offer in the following terms: 'O Abu Sufyan! You have constantly been plotting against Islam and the Muslims, but you cannot hurt them at all. Restrain yourself. As for us, we regard Abu Bakr as being worthy of it [the caliphate]' (Ibn Abiʾl-Hadid, *Sharh*, 6:40).

Abu Sufyan's incitement to ʿAli to rise up and fight for his rights is also reported in al-Zubayr b. Bakkar's *al-*

Muwaffaqiyyat. 'Ali's rebuttal of Abu Sufyan is expressed here by means of a poem as follows: 'You seek to involve us in an affair which is not appropriate for us. I have been entrusted with a covenant (*'ahd*) by the Messenger of God, and I am faithful to it' (cited by Ibn Abi'l-Hadid, *Sharh*, 6:17–18). One is reminded here of the 'bequest' discussed above.

'Ali's attitude to Abu Bakr's rule can be seen as extending to 'Umar also. As Madelung notes, 'Ali 'refrained from criticising the first two caliphs, whose general conduct he at times praised highly' (Madelung, *Succession*, 150–151). Arguably the most important piece of evidence corroborating the view that 'Ali sincerely accepted the legitimacy of the rule of Abu Bakr and 'Umar is the statement made by 'Ali when the council (*shura*) established by 'Umar to determine who was to succeed him had decided in favour not of 'Ali, but of 'Uthman. The fact that this statement is recorded in the *Nahj al-balagha* adds to its significance: 'You are all well aware that I am the most entitled (*ahaqqu*) to this [the caliphate]. But by God, I shall resign myself [to this situation] for as long as the affairs of the Muslims are being soundly governed (*ma salimat umur al-muslimin*), and for as long as there be no injustice except in relation to me alone. I do this, seeking the reward and the bounty of such a course of action, being detached from that to which you people aspire: the adornments and trappings [of political power]' (*Nahj*, Sermon no. 73, Ibn Abi'l-Hadid, *Sharh*, 6:166).

Although 'Ali is here speaking in the future tense in relation to the coming caliphate of 'Uthman—he *shall* resign himself for as long as the affairs of the Muslims are being soundly governed—the logic of his position can be applied retroactively to the rule of the previous caliphs as well. The implication here is that 'Ali probably viewed the rule of Abu Bakr and 'Umar as fundamentally benevolent and conducive to the general welfare of the Muslim community, even if he regarded both of them as less qualified than he to rule, less qualified in terms of knowledge—both in the formal, exoteric sciences, pertaining to the legal precepts explicit and implicit in the Qur'an and the Sunna, and as regards the esoteric knowledge of these twin sources of the Islamic revelation, together with the spiritual and mystical dimensions of the inner life.

The relative 'injustice' he suffered in relation to being subjected to less qualified persons than himself was deemed tolerable by 'Ali if the basic character of the rule of the caliphs was governed by sound Islamic principles. One observes that in relation to 'Uthman's rule, 'Ali's quiescent and passive attitude came to an end as soon as the affairs of the Muslims were seen to be governed badly. 'Ali remained 'resigned' to the status quo until the religio-political order deteriorated to the point that he felt obliged to intervene in political affairs in a way that he evidently never deemed necessary during the reigns of Abu Bakr and 'Umar. Referring back to the rule of all three caliphs in a letter appointing Qays b. Sa'd as governor of Egypt, 'Ali makes a distinction between the rule of the two 'righteous leaders' who succeeded the Prophet, and the third, who introduced 'innovations' (*ahdath*) which led to popular protests against him.

According to most reports, the second half of 'Uthman's rule was marred by the corruption of many of his clansmen whom he had appointed as governors of different provinces. This corruption led to widespread popular protests and also resulted in serious criticisms by senior companions such as 'Ammar b. Yasir, Abu Dharr al-Ghifari, Talha, Zubayr, and even 'Aisha, who voiced some of the most violent denunciations of 'Uthman on account of his treatment of the senior companions who dared to criticise his caliphate. 'Ali actively sought to assist 'Uthman put matters right, but with little success. However, one can argue that 'Ali's criticism of various actions of 'Uthman and his persistent efforts to persuade the latter to eliminate the 'innovations' that led to popular protests, signified not so much a withdrawal of support for 'Uthman's caliphate, but rather the opposite: 'Ali's wish to rectify the errors of the caliph was determined by a desire to restore the credibility and rectitude of a ruler whose fundamental political legitimacy he had recognised and affirmed through his *bay'a* to him. 'Ali's criticism of 'Uthman's policies was therefore constructive; as he is reported to have said shortly before 'Uthman was killed: 'By God, I have persisted in defending him until I am filled with shame. But Marwan, Mu'awiya, 'Abd Allah b. 'Amir and Sa'id b. al-'As [agents and supporters of 'Uthman's discredited policies] have dealt with him as you see. When I gave him sincere advice and directed him to send them away, he became suspicious of me.'

'Ali's constructive criticism of 'Uthman went hand in hand with strong opposition to any violent protests against the caliph. This was evident in his effort to protect 'Uthman against the rebels, going so far as to order his own sons, al-Hasan and al-Husayn, as well as his servant, Qanbar, to stand guard at the gates of 'Uthman's besieged residence, telling them to make sure that the rebels did not enter. When he was told that the rebels had overpowered these guards and killed 'Uthman, and that they then had regretted what they had done, 'Ali said, reciting from Q 59:16: 'Like Satan, when he said to man, "Disbelieve!"' The rest of the verse reads: 'Then, when he disbelieved, Satan said, "Surely I am quit of you. Surely, I fear God, Lord of all worlds".' The obvious implication here is that the rebels had been duped by satanic insinuation into performing a perfidious act.

In evaluating 'Ali's nuanced position on the caliphate, it is important to bear constantly in mind the distinction between political legitimacy and spiritual authority, a distinction which was later to be central to the practical implications of the Shi'i doctrine of the imamate. The distinction in question was brought out clearly in 'Ali's refusal to accept unequivocally the condition set by 'Abd al-Rahman b. 'Awf during the *shura* for assuming the caliphate, namely: that as caliph 'Ali would abide by the Qur'an, the *sunna* of the Prophet, and the precedents established by both Abu Bakr and 'Umar. According to most reports, 'Ali agreed to be bound only by the Qur'an and the *sunna*. 'Uthman's unambiguous acceptance of 'Abd al-Rahman's condition resulted in his being appointed caliph. 'Ali's position clearly manifests an element of disagreement with certain actions and policies of Abu Bakr and 'Umar, even if these disagreements were not such as would undermine, in 'Ali's eyes, the political legitimacy of the rule of the two caliphs. In addition to disagreements on the purely political plane, 'Ali's refusal to be bound by the precedents set by Abu Bakr and 'Umar is clearly related to his conviction that his own religious mandate and spiritual authority not only rendered such political precedents redundant; they also transcended the plane of politics altogether. This attitude led to the later articulation of the distinction between the spiritual authority of the imam and the political right of the imam in the doctrine of Ja'far al-Sadiq: while the spiritual authority of the imam to provide guidance is unconditional, and is thus to be exercised in all circumstances, the political right of the imam to rule is conditional, being contingent upon the requisite external circumstances.

This distinction between spiritual authority and temporal power was also implicit in another saying of 'Ali during the *shura*. When 'Abd al-Rahman asked all the members of the council to delegate to him the responsibility of choosing the successor to 'Umar, 'Ali said: 'We are the house of prophethood, the essence of wisdom, the safe haven for the inhabitants of the earth, and the means of salvation for those who seek it. Ours is the right [to the caliphate] whether we are granted it and decide to accept it, or whether we are denied it.' The implication here is that the spiritual authority to guide is not contingent upon the political right to rule; the function of political governance may or may not be exercised by the imam, whereas his spiritual prerogatives translate into a function which transcends the political domain and can be exercised whatever be the outward circumstances.

Before turning to the Imam's caliphate, let us give the following incident as one example of the way in which he assisted his predecessors in the caliphate. During 'Umar's rule, a man's wife delivered a child after just six months of marriage, and the man lodged an accusation of adultery against her. His wife accepted the fact that she had given birth to the child only six months after her marriage, but she insisted that her husband was indeed the father of her child. 'Umar ordered that she be punished, but 'Ali intervened. First, he cited from the Qur'an, 46:15: 'the bearing of the (child) to his weaning is (a period of) thirty months'; then he cited from 31:14: 'in travail upon travail did his mother bear him, and in two years was his weaning....' He concluded: if two years are deducted from thirty months, then a period of six months is left as a possible duration of a woman's pregnancy. After hearing this irrefutable argument, 'Umar famously declared: 'Were it not for 'Ali, 'Umar would indeed have perished' (Ibn 'Abd al-Barr, Isti'ab, 3:1103). The well-known saying of the Prophet, 'The most knowledgeable amongst you as regards passing judgement is 'Ali,' was repeatedly reiterated by the senior companions after the passing away of the Prophet. A telling report in this regard is the following: according to Sa'id ibn al-Musayyib, 'Umar used to pray to God to preserve him from having to confront any complicated problem (mu'dila) without the help of 'Ali (Ibn 'Abd al-Barr, Isti'ab, 3:1102–1103).

Finally, on the subject of Imam 'Ali's attitude to his predecessors in the caliphate, let us hear an apocryphal story, but which could well be true, and which also shows the Imam's sense of humour. During his caliphate, the Imam was approached by a man who said to him: 'How is it, O Commander of the Faithful, that under the Shaykhayn ('the two shaykhs', that is, Abu Bakr and 'Umar) we had nothing but the unity of Muslims, and the glory of Islam, but under you we have nothing but civil war?' The Imam replied: 'Because the *Shaykhayn* had people like me to consult, whereas I only have people like you!'

The Caliphate of Imam 'Ali (35–40/656–661)

The historical chronicles of Imam 'Ali's short caliphate of four and a half years are dominated by three civil wars; but the enduring hallmark of his caliphate was the principle of justice, to which he adhered with adamantine fidelity. His refusal to compromise on this fundamental principle was apparent at the very beginning of his rule. His first major undertaking as caliph was to replace the corrupt governors who had disgraced themselves and brought Islam into disrepute. He disregarded the advice he received from individuals such as Mughira b. Shuba and Ibn al-'Abbas, who were of the opinion that he should retain the previous governors until his position as caliph was consolidated, and then dismiss them. 'I do not doubt that this would be best for the sake of reconciliation in this world,' he replied, 'but there is my obligation to the Truth, and my knowledge of 'Uthman's governors—so, by God, I shall never appoint one of them.' Here we see that the Imam was not prepared to maintain the unity of the Muslim community at *any* price: he did not countenance corruption, nepotism or abuse of power for a single moment, and was compelled by his duty to the Truth to dismiss corrupt governors even at the risk of splitting the Muslim community.

This decisive act at the outset of his caliphate has been characterised by certain historians as naivety (see, for example, Madelung, *Succession*, 149–150), an excessively rigid adherence to principle, an ignorance of the subtle requirements of political pragmatism, or an inability to adopt the prophetic mode of governance—that combination of spiritual principle and psychological realism by which the Prophet made erstwhile enemies into stalwart allies. These failures, so it has been argued, plunged the nascent Muslim polity into civil war. However, it is possible to argue that what the Imam did was the only possible course of action open to him, both on principle and in practice. On principle, it was inconceivable for him to act in any other way, given his adherence to the Truth at all levels. In addition, from the purely pragmatic point of view, had he acted in any other way, he would have undermined the moral basis of his own legitimacy, and would have been seen by his supporters as compromising Islamic principle for the sake of short-term political advantage. When the Prophet allowed former enemies such as Abu Sufyan to retain their positions of wealth and status after converting to Islam, and took advantage of their proven leadership qualities, this was done to give them a chance to prove that their official 'conversion' to the outward forms of Islam went hand in hand with an adoption of its ethical values. The governors whom Imam 'Ali was dealing with—such as the son of Abu Sufyan, that is, Mu'awiya—were, by contrast, those who had been given immense power and proved themselves incapable of resisting the temptations offered by that power, year after year. To give such thoroughly discredited, corrupt politicians yet another chance would be tantamount to overlooking their corruption and fatally undermining the Imam's own ethical credibility and political legitimacy.

According to the pragmatic side of this argument, the Imam's own power base in Medina, consisting in no small measure of the rebels who had overthrown the previous caliphate in the name of justice, would have turned against him if he had shown any willingness to compromise with the very governors whose corruption had led to the uprising in the first place. Had he not dismissed these corrupt governors immediately, the widespread popular outrage resulting from their corrupt policies would doubtless have become more intense, thus resulting in further social and political instability.

Similarly, the Imam's act of distributing equally among the population all the wealth in the public treasury has been regarded by some as 'imprudent', whereas for his supporters this act is upheld as a socio-economic expression of his sense of justice. Indeed, this was one of the chief features of his fiscal policy—signalling a return to the precedent of both the Prophet and the first caliph—in contrast to that of his two predecessors in the caliphate. 'Umar had instituted a gradation of payments from the public treasury based on merit, while 'Uthman had allowed the inequalities thus generated to become even more acute by tolerating or turning a blind eye to the systematic abuse of public funds perpetrated by members of his clan. The gross inequalities of wealth with which the Imam was confronted needed to be addressed swiftly, decisively and uncompromisingly, both for the sake of justice and, on the plane of pragmatism, in order to diminish the divisive and revolutionary tendencies that such inequalities and injustices inevitably produce.

The Battle of Jamal

The first challenge to the Imam's rule arose from two senior companions of the Prophet, Talha b. 'Ubayd Allah and al-Zubayr b. al-'Awwam, together with 'Aisha and other officials who had been ousted by Imam 'Ali. They accused the new caliph of failing to punish the murderers of 'Uthman, and justified their revolt under the banner of just vengeance for the murdered caliph. Imam 'Ali reminded Talha and al-Zubayr that they had made an oath of allegiance to him, which they were now violating, and he insisted that he would bring the murderers to justice as soon as he could find them. But to no avail: the ensuing battle, which took place near Basra, on

15 Jumada al-Ula 36/8 December 656, was the first civil war of Islam. It was named *al-Jamal* (The Camel) after the camel litter of 'Aisha which became the focus of the fighting. It resulted in the victory of the Imam's army, the death of Talha (killed treacherously by his own ally, Marwan b. al-Hakam, who held Talha personally responsible for the murder of the caliph 'Uthman), the death of al-Zubayr (killed also by one of his allies, after fleeing from the battlefield) and 'Aisha's surrender.

Two points about this battle should be noted. First, it was just before it commenced that Imam 'Ali imparted one of his most esoteric teachings on the meaning of *tawhid*. A bedouin came to him and asked: 'O Commander of the Faithful! Do you say that God is one?' Those present remonstrated with the bedouin, telling him to leave his question for later, when the Imam was less preoccupied. However, Imam 'Ali said: 'Leave him alone, for surely what the bedouin wishes is what we wish for the people.' For the Imam there was no time when such a question could be called unimportant: his metaphysical contemplation was not left at home when he went out to fight a battle in self-defence. Rather, action and contemplation were in complete harmony, as they were both aimed at upholding, defending and establishing the Truth. It was for the sake of the correct knowledge of God, and in defence of the ethical repercussions of this knowledge in society, that the Imam was fighting. On the very field of battle, then, in the manner of a Krishna imparting the Bhagavad Gita to Arjuna at the field of Kurukshetra, he delivers a discourse on the meaning of divine oneness. The first part of this contains a key to the understanding of his whole spiritual ethos. He refutes the notion of God's oneness as being in any way a 'numerical' or 'countable' oneness, and tells the bedouin that it is not permissible to think of divine unity while having in mind any numerical conception. In one of his most stunning expressions of *tawhid*—again, reminding us of Hindu wisdom, this time the key principle of Advaita, or 'non-duality'—he says: 'That which has no second (*ma la thaniya lahu*) does not enter into the category of number.'

We have here one instance of Imam 'Ali's 'fight' for *ta'wil*, as prophesied by the Prophet. The fact that the teaching is given on the battlefield is significant. He ignores the enemy ranged opposite him, and instead imparts a teaching pertaining to the metaphysical essence of *tawhid*: the meaning of *la ilaha illa'Llah*, no god but God, is taken from the conventional plane of theology to the metaphysical plane of Being. This is not just a question of denying the existence of other gods alongside God; rather, it is about appreciating that, apart from God, nothing else has authentic being. 'That which has no second' means that there is no reality, ultimately, but the one and only Reality: everything other than God is, in the last analysis, an illusion.

We also engage here with another symbolism, that of the 'greatest battle', *al-jihad al-akbar*. Given that the teaching is imparted on the field of battle, we can read this discourse as a commentary on the Prophet's famous declaration, after returning from a battle, that 'We have returned from the lesser *jihad* to the greater *jihad*.' When asked what this greater *jihad* was, he replied: 'the *jihad* of the soul.' The inner battle against one's own vices and shortcomings is much more difficult, and more subtle, than any struggle against an external foe. Putting these ideas together, we may see that the 'fight' for *ta'wil* is linked to the greater *jihad*; that is, the war that must be waged against the enemy within.

Secondly, this account points to the Imam's magnanimity towards his defeated foes. Here we should remember the image, described in Chapter 1, by which he demonstrates how to triumph in the 'greater *jihad*': within the soul, the intellect (*'aql*) is the commander of the forces of *al-Rahman* (the Infinitely Compassionate); while egoistic desire (*hawa*) is the commander of the forces of *al-Shaytan* (the Devil). It is God's compassion, mercy and love which empower the intellect in its struggle against egotism. As mentioned earlier, Imam 'Ali's designation as the archetypal *fata*, or chivalric knight, has much more to do with his perceived magnanimity and compassion than his skill as a warrior. We see this clearly in the way he treated his defeated opponents at the Battle of Jamal. Zubayr's killer was triumphantly brought before the Imam. The man was expecting a great reward, but instead Imam 'Ali looked away, and said he had heard from the Prophet that the man who was to kill Zubayr would go to hell. He then said that Zubayr was a good man, but that 'circumstances had prevailed over him.' He recited the following verse, saying that he hoped that the principle expressed in the verse would apply to him and to Talha and Zubayr: 'We shall remove from their breasts whatever bitterness they have towards each other [so they shall be like] brothers upon thrones face to face [in Paradise]' (Q 15:47).

This extraordinary manifestation of magnanimity, wisdom and compassion is recorded in both Sunni and Shi'i sources (see, for example, Ibn Abi Shayba, *Musannaf*, 14:263). Imam 'Ali, instead of vilifying and dehumanising one's enemy in war—a psychological tendency all too familiar in the history of warfare worldwide—prayed that he might encounter his erstwhile enemies in Paradise, all bitterness having been taken from their souls by God. In making this supplication, he also taught us that great men, even those destined for Paradise, can make great mistakes in the life of this lower world. One may, regrettably, have to fight in self-defence against such people, but one must never fail to be objective about their good qualities, nor fail to show mercy and compassion to them whenever possible, most especially in the wake of victory over them. In one's estimation of the opponent, one must always ensure that his essential qualities prevail over any secondary or accidental faults. And one must always be oriented towards the mercy of God. As the Imam says, in one of the aphorisms recorded in the *Nahj al-balagha*, 'When you overpower your enemy, make your forgiveness of him an expression of gratitude for having prevailed over him.' Finally, one must pray that one's opponents be forgiven rather than damned. When the Imam heard one of his supporters cursing Mu'awiya at Siffin, he said to him, 'Pray, instead, that he be guided.'

It is to be noted in this connection that Imam 'Ali refused to allow his soldiers to take as booty the property of the defeated Muslims. They were not 'enemies' whose property could be confiscated; rather, they had rebelled against legitimate state authority, but they must still be treated as Muslims, who were to be pardoned once they had been defeated, and then given the right to resume their normal lives upon the termination of hostilities. This principle was to become the basis of legal codes that were enshrined in books of law pertaining to warfare among Muslims.

Again, in relation to 'Aisha, Imam 'Ali's conduct was both forgiving and chivalrous. First, he ensured that her own brother, Muhammad b. Abi Bakr, who was fighting on 'Ali's side, would be the person to carry her from her felled litter, so preventing her from being touched by a soldier who was unrelated to her. Secondly, he pardoned 'Aisha unconditionally, allowing her to return to Medina and live in dignity for the rest of her life. This is a lesson in Muslim *adab* (propriety and etiquette), shedding further light on why the Imam has been regarded throughout Muslim history as the exemplar of the noble knight. He had forty women accompany 'Aisha back to Medina, but in order to protect her against any acts of retaliation, he ordered they should be disguised in armour, thus appearing to be men. Throughout the journey, 'Aisha thought that a troop of men was guarding her. When she realised, upon arrival at Medina, what 'Ali had done, she exclaimed: 'May God reward 'Ali ibn Abi Talib well, for he has safeguarded the sanctity of the Messenger of God through me [through protecting my honour]' (Mufid, *Camel*, 432). Here we see an instance of the principle referred to in the Qur'an as follows: 'The beautiful deed and the evil deed are not alike. Repel [the evil deed] with one that is most beautiful, and behold: your enemy will become like a bosom friend' (41:34). The Imam's magnanimity towards 'Aisha, despite the leading role she played in the battle, appears to have brought about a state of deep repentance in her soul. In one of her expressions of repentance, she said that, had God offered her the choice between bearing ten sons for the Prophet, or not fighting 'Ali at Jamal, she would have chosen the latter.

Finally, let us ponder what Imam 'Ali meant when he referred to future generations 'witnessing' the battle. One of his companions came to him and said how sorry he was that one of his friends, fighting on the side of the Imam, had been killed in the battle and had not lived to witness their victory. The Imam said to him: your friend did indeed witness it, and so did people 'who are still in the loins of men and the wombs of women, who will be brought into this world in the future' (Sermon 12, *Nahj*). The Imam is graced with a vision which pierces the veil of duration, allowing him to see certain things *sub specie aeternitatis* ('from the point of view of eternity'; see the discussion of the prophet's deathbed transmission of knowledge in the previous chapter). The mysterious flow of time is arrested and synthesised, allowing him, by the grace of God, to see future events with the 'eye of the heart'.

Mu'awiya and the Battle of Siffin

Imam 'Ali now turned to face the next challenge, the rebellion of Mu'awiya, governor of Syria, who was dismissed from his post by the Imam, but defied this command from the new caliph. Instead, like Talha and Zubayr, Mu'awiya used the claim of seeking vengeance for 'Uthman as the pretext for opposing Imam 'Ali. Following minor skirmishes at Siffin, all-out hostilities began on 8 Safar 37/26 July 657. After some days, and much bloodshed on both sides, the Imam's army was on the point of victory. Mu'awiya then received the cunning advice of his chief advisor, 'Amr b. al-'As, to hoist copies of the Qur'an on spears and appeal for arbitration 'according to God's Word.' Though clearly a ruse, many in Imam 'Ali's army who were lukewarm in their support for his cause laid down their arms; led by Ash'ath b. Qays, the most powerful tribal chief of Kufa, they insisted on accepting this call for arbitration. Imam 'Ali was also compelled by the same elements within his ranks to appoint Abu Musa al-Ash'ari as his representative in the arbitration. Mu'awiya appointed 'Amr as his representative.

The text of the arbitration agreement was drawn up on 15 Safar 37/2 August 657. It called for the arbitrators to arrive at a decision binding on all, doing so on the basis of the Qur'an, and to resort to the prophetic Sunna (conduct) if they were unable to find the necessary ruling in the Qur'an. They were to seek peace, but apart from that no other matter for arbitration was specifically mentioned. The arbitrators met at Dumat al-Jandal for about three weeks in the spring of 658. This meeting was held against the background of increasing discontent in the ranks of 'Ali's army. Many of those who had initially supported the arbitration now felt that it was not only an error to have resorted to arbitration, it was also a sin; it was tantamount to leaving to men the right that pertained only to God, whence their cry: 'no judgement but that of God' (la hukm illa li-Llah). Although 'Ali succeeded, through patient dialogue, in bringing most of the malcontents back into the fold at this stage, the seeds of a wider rebellion were sown.

The arbitration process was almost immediately under-mined by 'Amr's proposal that the issue of 'Uthman's inno-cence of erroneous 'innovations' be decided before anything else. This effectively changed the focus of the arbitration, for once it was decided that 'Uthman had been wrongfully killed, the legitimacy of Mu'awiya's claim for revenge was upheld, and 'Ali's culpability in failing to bring the killers of 'Uthman to justice was implied. Imam 'Ali saw through the ruse, and dismissed the whole arbitration process. When he proceeded to call his men to arms, he was confronted by the growing ranks of those who came to be called the 'Khawarij' (anglicised as 'Kharijites'); literally, those who 'departed' from Imam 'Ali's army, but in this context meaning the 'seceders'. They demanded that 'Ali repent of the 'sin' of having accepted the arbitration proposal in the first place, as they themselves had repented. When he failed to repent, they accused him of being not just a sinner but also a disbeliever. According to their twisted logic, the taking of 'Ali's life, and of all those who supported him, was now lawful. Imam 'Ali did everything possible to dissuade them from fighting, and entered into long discussions with their leaders. As a result of this policy of patient dialogue, a large number of the seceders were reconciled, but the hard core resisted and resolved to fight to the finish.

Given the murderous tactics used by this group against 'Ali's supporters, and their declaration that all those who opposed them were *kafirs* (unbelievers) and thus must be killed, 'Ali had no choice but to fight them, despite his great reluctance to wage yet another battle. What made this conflict all the more bitter was that the Kharijites numbered in their ranks a significant group of apparently pious souls, known as the *qurra'*, the Qur'an-readers, on account of their knowledge of, and dedication to, Qur'an recitation. But this outward show of piety went hand in hand with fanaticism and violence. When asked about these apparently pious people who prayed long hours each night, 'Ali said: 'Sleeping with certainty is better than praying with doubt'—implying with the word 'doubt' the voice of spiritual conscience that was trying to break through the shrill tones of self-righteousness uttered by the outwardly religious *qurra'*.

Imam 'Ali now had to confront this violent form of religious hypocrisy. After much time spent in dialogue with the Kharijites, their ranks were reduced to about 1,500 men who were led by 'Abd Allah b. Wahb. The resulting battle at Nahrawan, in Dhu'l-Hijja 37/May 658, resulted in their defeat and dispersal. The point to be stressed here is that, yet again, Imam 'Ali resorted to patient dialogue, reducing the ranks of his diehard opponents by thousands. It was only when they fanatically insisted on fighting that he was forced to defend himself. We shall return to this point below.

Returning to the arbitration process, the final stage, held at Adhruh in Shaban 38/January 659, was brought to an end, as it had been initiated in the first place, by one of 'Amr's ruses: he proposed to Abu Musa that they both depose their respective masters and then set up a council to appoint the new caliph. Abu Musa agreed, and duly 'deposed' 'Ali, upon which 'Amr immediately declared Mu'awiya the sole caliph. This declaration was of course rejected by Imam 'Ali, who subsequently prepared once again for a resumption of hostilities. However, before he was able to regroup his forces, he was mortally wounded by Ibn Muljam, one of the Kharijites, in the congregational mosque of Kufa, on 19 Ramadan 40/26 January 661, dying two days later. Even when mortally wounded and in great pain, 'Ali was compassionate: he noticed that Ibn Muljam's hands were bleeding, and told those who had bound him to loosen the bonds around his wrists. Later on, he told those responsible for Ibn Muljam to make sure that they treated him well: 'Give him good food and a soft bed,' he said.

Before he died, the Imam composed a valedictory letter of advice to his son, Hasan. It is a long letter, full of inspiring advice, sobering admonition and wise maxims. The following short extract gives us a taste of this document, as priceless as it is timeless:

I admonish you to have constant awareness of God

(*taqwa*), O my son, to abide by His commandments, to fill your heart with His remembrance (*dhikrihi*), and to cling to the rope He has held out to you [see Q 3:103]; for no protection is greater than that which extends from Him to you—provided you take hold of His rope [with absolute trust]. Enliven your heart with exhortation (*maw'iza*), mortify it by renunciation (*zahada*), empower it with certainty (*yaqin*), enlighten it with wisdom, humble it by the remembrance of death (*dhikr al-mawt*), establish it in [constant awareness of] the evanescence (*fana'*) [of all things other than God]... (Jibouri, *Path of Eloquence*, 275; translation modified).

◆

He who seeks Me, finds Me; he who finds Me, knows Me; he who knows Me, loves Me; he who loves Me, I love him; he whom I love, I slay; he whom I slay, I must requite; he whom I must requite, I myself am his requital.

Thus does God reveal, according to Imam 'Ali, the reality linking death and love. God Himself takes the place of the one He 'slays': the idea here is that divine love consumes all that is other than itself, just as a fire consumes and makes one with itself the wood that it burns. The 'death' of the wood is the other side of the coin of its becoming one with the fire. Thus, apparent death is translated into eternal life, or rather, eternal love.

We have insisted that Imam 'Ali's life was a triumph of the human spirit over the tragedies and absurdities which are unavoidable in this world. But his words, as he was struck by the poisoned sword of Ibn Muljam take us away from human misery to divine mercy, from a tragic fatality to the nectar of immortality, from the historical fact of a man's apparent death to the timeless mystery of his eternal life: 'I have triumphed,' the Imam cried out instantaneously, 'by the Lord of the Ka'ba!'

Imam 'Ali had 'triumphed' at the point of death because the whole of his life had in fact already been a triumph even if, from the worldly point of view, the historical record may indicate otherwise. This undefeated champion of Islam never before made such an utterance after any of his many extraordinary 'triumphs' on the field of battle. Only now, after being treacherously struck on the head while prostrate in prayer, did he make such a statement, as paradoxical to the worldly minded as it is profound to those with a sense of eternity. He had triumphed because, throughout his life, it was that which lay beyond this life that had sustained him, as a mother's milk sustains the life of her suckling babe: he was more intimate with death, he said, than is the babe with the breast of its mother. In fact, this saying should be quoted verbatim, for he describes himself as 'the son of Abu Talib', as if referring to somebody else, thereby rhetorically reinforcing the detachment and self-effacement implicit in this powerful oath: 'I swear,' he says, 'that the son of Abu Talib is more intimate with death than is the babe with the breast of its mother.'

This is far from any morbid fixation on death as negation; rather, it bears eloquent testimony to the fact that Imam 'Ali was already in a mysterious sense 'dead to the world', not out of an indifference to this lower domain, but because his spiritual life, the life of his 'heart', was already reverberating inwardly in Paradise. 'Even if the veil be removed, I could not increase in certainty,' he said. The 'veil' is everything 'other than God,' the life of this world, including pre-eminently the phenomenon of death. 'Die before you die,' said the Prophet, which can be read as a comment on these words of Jesus, according to the Gospel of St Luke (17:33): 'Whosoever seeks to save his life shall lose it; and whosoever shall lose his life shall preserve it.' Likewise, we have this profound spiritual statement by Shakespeare, through the persona of the Duke in *Measure for Measure*: 'Be absolute for death; either death or life shall thereby be the sweeter' (Act 3, scene 1).

It is not death as fatal negation that Imam 'Ali is so intimate with, but rather life after death, thus, physical death only inasmuch as it is the threshold of eternal life: when he says that he is more intimate with death than is the suckling babe with the breast of its mother, he is affirming an as it were 'organic' intimacy, not with death as such, but with the beautiful reality that lies beyond the veil of death. 'If you want to see a dead man walking,' said the Prophet, 'then look at 'Ali.' And Imam 'Ali said about himself: 'The pathways of Heaven are more known to me than those on earth'; and in another saying alluded to above, he affirms that he belongs to a group of saints 'whose hearts are already in the Garden, only their bodies are at work in this world.' To say that his heart was already in the Garden of Paradise is to say (among other things) that, even while in this world, his inmost consciousness was penetrated by an already celestial quality, such that he was capable of not only seeing Paradise within himself, but also witnessing it in the world: that is, he could see through the phenomena of this world to the paradisal archetypes which they manifest symbolically. 'There is no thing,' the Qur'an says, in an explicit description of the divine archetypes that are the source of all positive qualities, in Paradise and on earth, 'but that its treasuries are with Us; and We only send it down in a known measure' (15:21). And again: 'Every time they [the dwellers of Paradise] are given to eat from the fruit of the Garden, they say: this is what we were given to eat before [i.e., on earth]' (2:25). Imam 'Ali was one who was given a foretaste of the fruit of Paradise already on earth. As mentioned above, the Imam had been granted an inward liberation from earthly suffering because he had vanquished his ego—and when the ego is vanquished, the heart is graced with inner peace, a prolongation of celestial serenity.

According to tradition, the Prophet had told Imam 'Ali the

identity of the person who would kill him. In his poetic vision, Rumi describes the spiritual state of Imam 'Ali with regard to his death:

> Day and night I see the murderer with my eyes, (but) I have no anger against him, because death has become sweet as manna to me: my death has laid fast hold of resurrection.
>
> 'Tis death outwardly but life inwardly: apparently 'tis a cutting-off, in secret (in reality) 'tis permanence (life without end).
>
> To the embryo in the womb birth is a going (to another state of existence): in the world it (the embryo) blossoms anew.
>
> Slay me, my trusty friends [an Arabic citation from a famous poem by Hallaj], slay me, vile as I am: verily, in my being slain is my life for evermore.
> (Rumi, *Mathnawi* 1:3925ff.)

Principles of Just Governance

Some instances of Imam 'Ali's adherence to justice in the political and legal domains have been noted above. His rulings, sayings and attitudes establish clear principles for policies relating to religious tolerance. For example, in what was to become one of the most influential treatises on sound governance in the entire Islamic tradition—his letter to Malik al-Ashtar, appointing him governor of Egypt—he writes:

> Infuse your heart with mercy for the subjects, love for them and kindness towards them. Be not like a ravenous beast of prey above them, seeking to devour them. For they are of two types: either your brother in religion or your equal in creation. Mistakes slip from them, defects emerge from them, deliberately or accidentally. So bestow

upon them your forgiveness and your pardon, just as you would have God bestow upon you His forgiveness and pardon; for you are above them, and the one who appointed you as governor is above you, and God is above him who appointed you... and through them He tests you [see Shah-Kazemi 2006, Appendix 2, for an annotated translation of this letter].

The theme of justice to all—of whatever religion—is here intertwined with the principle of compassion. This passage of the letter remains to this day one of the most important and explicit articulations of the principle of the essential unity of the human race, and the consequent equality of all human beings. It is a powerful antidote against the poison of religious prejudice. Drawing the link between the quality of compassion and the nature of God enables us to see more clearly the spiritual (not just moral) perversion constituted by injustice and oppression. Compassion is an essential expression of justice, far from being separate or distinct from it: justice is at one with God's very nature, and this nature is intrinsically merciful. Imam 'Ali asserts, in one of his sermons: 'I bear witness that He [God] is Justice ['adl] and He acts justly.' On the other hand, according to the Qur'an: God has inscribed mercy on His own Self (6:12 and 6:54); His mercy encompasses all things (7:156); and, for this very reason, He rewards good deeds tenfold but punishes sin only with its equivalent (see, for example, 6:160). It is for this reason that the true *faqih* ('one who understands'; by extension, the 'jurist') is defined by the Imam, most revealingly, as 'he who never makes people despair of the mercy of God.' Likewise, one should note the following sayings, which help to reveal his perspective on just governance:

⬦ The dispensing of mercy brings down [divine] mercy.

⬦ As you grant mercy, so will you be granted mercy.

⋄ I am astounded by the person who hopes for mercy from one above him, while he is not merciful to those beneath him.

Also contained in the letter to Malik is the following instruction pertaining to military commanders. It discloses something most revealing about 'Ali b. Abi Talib himself: the compassionate heart of the chivalric knight, the *fata* of Islam par excellence, is describing himself through this instruction to Malik. One recalls the description of the 'guardians' given in Plato's *Republic*: their military training is to go hand in hand with philosophical, ethical and even aesthetic training, since the hearts of the defenders have to be softened, even while their bodies are to be toughened:

Appoint as the commander of your soldiers the person whom you feel deeply is the most sincere in relation to God, the Prophet and your Imam, the purest of heart, the one most excellent in forbearance (*hilm*); who is slow to anger, happy to pardon, kind to the weak, severe with the strong; one who is neither moved by violence, nor held back by weakness. Cleave to those of noble descent, belonging to pious families of established name and repute, and to men known for their bravery, courage, generosity and tolerance.

This combination of indomitable strength and gentle compassion well describes Imam 'Ali's own disposition. As briefly mentioned above, Imam 'Ali was known for this rare combination of qualities. One of his companions, Sa'sa'a b. Suhan, describes him as follows: 'He was amongst us as one of our own, of gentle disposition (*lin janib*), intense humility, leading with a light touch (*suhulat qiyad*), even though we were in awe of him with the kind of awe that a bound prisoner has before one who holds a sword over his head' (Ibn Abi'l-Hadid, *Sharh*, 1:25). Imam 'Ali was renowned for the charismatic ease of his character (*sajahat al-akhlaq*) and the joyfulness of his

104

countenance (*bishr al-wajh*). Ibn Abi'l-Hadid wrote, in his commentary on the *Nahj*, that 'these qualities of his became proverbial, so much so that his enemies construed them as faults.' So 'light' was his touch, so gentle his disposition, and so radiant his inward joy, that in the propaganda war preceding the Battle of Siffin, 'Amr accused him of being lighthearted in a kind of playful and frivolous way (using the word *du'aba*). When he was told what was being said about him by 'Amr, he retorted: 'By God, the remembrance of death prevents me from such playfulness, while forgetfulness of the Hereafter prevents him from speaking the truth' (Ibn Abi'l-Hadid, *Sharh*, 6:280).

Imam 'Ali's remembrance of death also meant that his espousal of the principles of mercy and compassion did not prevent him from meting out appropriate punishment to officials found guilty of corruption whenever it was necessary. His insistence on tolerance did not extend to corruption: for example, he forcefully exercised a policy of 'zero tolerance' for any kind of misappropriation of public funds. In his letter to Malik, he tells him to inflict severe punishment upon any official found guilty of abuse of his authority. And in a letter to Ziyad b. Abihi, deputy to the governor of Basra, he issues this stern warning:

> I swear by God an oath in all sincerity: if news reaches me that you have misappropriated the revenue of the Muslims, whether a small or large amount, I shall inflict a severe punishment upon you, one which will lighten your wealth, crush your back, and degrade you.

In a threat of punishment to another governor guilty of misappropriation of assets, Imam 'Ali said: 'By God, even if Hasan and Husayn had done the like of what you have done, they would not have been granted any leniency by me.' Nobody, whatever their prestige, has the right to infringe on the rights of others. In one of his sermons, the Imam refers to

105

an inappropriate request for public funds made to him by his blind brother, 'Aqil. He replied by taking his brother's hand close to a red-hot iron, and saying that, were he to comply with this request, he would enter into a much more intense fire. Instead of taking money from the public treasury, Imam 'Ali gave his brother some of his own income from his private estate in Yanbu.

Needless to say, Imam 'Ali led by personal example, making a sharp distinction between the public and the private domain. One evening, when working by the light of a candle on affairs of the state, two people came to ask him a question. The Imam wanted to know whether the matter was official or personal. When told it was personal, he snuffed out the candle, and lit a different one. They asked why he had done this; the Imam replied that when he worked on official business, he used a candle that belonged to the state treasury, but when he worked on private affairs, he used one of his own candles.

Another example: he refused to eat anything other than coarse bread and the simplest of food; when asked why he was so strict with himself, he replied: 'God has made it incumbent on true leaders (*a'immat al-haqq*) to make themselves commensurable with (*yuqaddiru anfusahum*) the weakest people over whom they rule, so that the poverty of the poor will not engender covetousness.' Here we have an inspiring lesson on the need for the most powerful to identify with the most powerless in their domain. Can one think of a more effective way of diminishing worldliness and materialism in society than this deliberate adoption by its leaders of a life of austerity and simplicity, when these leaders have the power to live in the lap of luxury? He who could have the most chooses to have the least, is content with it, and publicly displays his contentment with it. In this manner, the 'true leader' radiates spiritual values, thereby providing a powerful antidote to the poisons of materialism, greed, jealousy and bitterness.

The Imam is here implying that if a leader is to be among

the *a'immat al-haqq*, the true leaders, he must manifest his attachment to *al-Haqq*, the Real (one of the Names of God), in the light of which material wealth is of little consequence. Thus, as the most powerful man in the land, he shares with the powerless and the poor the most important treasure of all: the infinite riches of the spiritual domain, one of the most beautiful jewels of which is contentment. According to one of the Imam's aphorisms, as found in the *Nahj*: 'Contentment is wealth which does not diminish.' Contentment with what one has goes hand in hand with an absence of desire for what one does not have: 'The greatest wealth is the absence of hope for what others possess.'

Contentment is closely related to another jewel in the infinite treasuries of the spiritual domain: knowledge. In his famous discourse to Kumayl, he says: 'O Kumayl, knowledge is better than wealth, for knowledge guards you, while you must guard wealth; wealth diminishes as it is spent, while knowledge increases as it is given to others; the results of wealth disappear with the disappearance of wealth... Knowledge is a judge, while wealth is judged.'

All have access to spiritual wealth, then, in proportion to their knowledge of the Truth, *al-Haqq*, derived from the Revelation of God, and their contentment, derived from heartfelt submission to God. With these spiritual values upheld, it will be easier to appreciate that all mankind is in a state of spiritual poverty in relation to God who, alone, can be called 'wealthy', for He is *al-Ghani*, 'The Infinitely Rich': 'O mankind, you are the poor before God, and God, He is the Infinitely Rich, the absolutely Praiseworthy' (Q 35:15).

◆

It should be noted that the Imam respected private property, and did not engage in any communist-style confiscation of private assets in an attempt to enforce a uniform standard of living upon all. Rather, he merely wished to mitigate the inevitable inequalities of wealth, to eliminate the exploitation and neglect of the poor by the wealthy, and ensure that the wealth of the rich was not increased at the expense of the further impoverishment of the poor. This was completely in accord with the verse of the Qur'an which warns against the danger of the wealth of the Muslims 'circulating only amongst the rich' (59:7). On the plane of social psychology, one should note the efficacy of the Imam's insistence upon rulers eschewing luxury, and instead living like the poor. It minimises the risk of material inequalities in society generating envy among the poor, while reminding the wealthy that they must not be ostentatious about their wealth, nor consider that their wealth bestows upon them any mark of distinction. It is an effective way of reminding us that the criterion of value—and the source of true nobility—is not material wealth but rather awareness of God, together with the virtues this spiritual awareness implies: 'O mankind, the most noble of you, in the eyes of God, are those among you who are most conscious of God' (Q 49:13).

Arguably, it was Imam 'Ali's fiscal policy that signified most clearly his desire to restore justice, through the elimination of the vast inequalities that had become entrenched in Muslim society, chiefly as a result of his predecessor's policies. In implementing the equal distribution of wealth to all Muslims—whether freed slaves of Persian origin or Arab tribal chieftains—he was reinstating the Prophet's policy (followed also by Abu Bakr, but not by 'Umar or 'Uthman), which recognised no hierarchy or stratification in respect of the distribution of the community's wealth. One of his advisors, 'Uthman b. Hunayf, warned him that by giving equal stipends to all, and depriving the wealthy Arab nobles of their special grants, he was losing the latter's support. They were abandoning him in favour of Mu'awiya, who was always ready to grant favours to the rich in return for their political support. By contrast, 'Uthman continued, those who benefited from the new policies—the poor, the disabled, the widows and the slaves—would provide no political advantage.

Imam 'Ali's response is well worth considering: as regards the deserters, he was happy that such people were leaving him; the implication being that those for whom accumulation of material wealth is the overriding aim in life were not people he would want in his camp. As regards the poor, whose rights he was upholding, his aim was not to benefit from their services; rather, it was he who wished to perform a service for them. He concluded with a prayer, asking God for help in the correct performance of this duty.

He wrote a famous letter (no. 45 in certain editions of the *Nahj*) to 'Uthman b. Hunayf, when the latter was governor of Basra. 'Uthman had accepted an invitation to an extravagantly sumptuous banquet, one which 'rudely rebuffed the needy, and warmly embraced the wealthy.' This elicited a strong remonstrance from the Imam. He wrote: 'Every follower (*ma'mum*) has a leader (*imam*) whom he follows and by the light of whose knowledge he is illumined. Do you not see that, as regards his world, your Imam is satisfied with two simple pieces of cloth, and as regards his food, with two loaves of bread? Doubtless this is beyond your capacity, but at least lend me your help in realising the virtues of restraint, exertion, modesty and propriety.'

He rhetorically asks 'Uthman how he, 'Ali, could go to bed with his belly full, while there are people around him who are hungry. He continues in this vein, alerting 'Uthman to the relationship between self-restraint and spiritual awareness, reminding him of the reason he was created, and finishing with a description of the true 'partisans of God' (*hizb Allah*):

> Can I possibly allow myself to be called 'Commander of the Faithful' (*Amir al-mu'minin*), if I do not share with them [i.e., the faithful] the adversities of fate, if I do not give them a role-model to emulate when confronted with the hardships of life? I was not created to be engrossed by

consumption of fine foods like a hobbled beast... Blessed
the person who discharges his obligations towards God;
struggles courageously against all misfortune; abandons
sleep at night, until, when slumber overpowers him, lies
down on the earth as his bed, using his hand as his
pillow, doing so in the company of those whose eyes
are rendered sleepless by awesome anticipation of their
return [to God]; whose bodies stay away from their beds
[see Q 32:16]; whose lips are ever-humming with the
invocation of the Name of their Lord; whose sins have
been dissolved through prolonged cries for forgiveness.
They are the 'partisans of God': 'verily the partisans of
God, they are the successful ones!' (Q 58:22). So fear God,
O son of Hunayf, and may your daily bread suffice you,
restraining you from greed, thus saving you from the Fire.

♦

Imam 'Ali was so insistent on the principle of strict equality in
the distribution of public revenue that, even when confronted
by the aggressive opposition of the Kharijites (who had
begun to insult him, disrupting the congregational prayers
he was leading in the mosque of Kufa, calling him a *kafir*
etc.), he continued to pay them their due from the public
treasury. When urged by his supporters to punish them for
their rebellious behaviour, he said that for as long as they
attacked him with their tongues he would defend himself with
his tongue; if they resorted to striking him with their hands,
he would defend himself with his hand; and only if they took
up arms against him would he draw his sword in self-defence.
In our troubled times of fanaticism assuming the guise of
religion, the Imam's confrontation, both martial and spiritual,
with the fanatics of his time takes on added significance, as
does his extraordinarily lenient behaviour towards them until
the resort to arms was forced upon him. Even when their
opposition to him was clear and intense, he never ceased

paying them their due from the public treasury, nor did he prevent them from giving vent to their opposition, so long as this was expressed only verbally. The inviolability of 'freedom of speech' is clearly implicit in the key principle defining his attitude as ruler towards the Kharijites: if their opposition was restricted to speech, the Imam's response would be verbal, and only if they resorted to arms would he do so in self-defence (see for discussion, Yusufiyan and Sharifi, 238–246). In other words, he allowed them to give vent to their grievances so long as their opposition to him was expressed only verbally. In modern parlance, he is clearly upholding the inviolability of the principle of freedom of speech. Instead of resorting to suppression of dissent, which would serve only to aggravate the sense of grievance against the ruler, he allowed people to express their differences of opinion, so long as this was done peacefully.

Another act of great significance, from the point of view of establishing a precedent in the domains of both redistributive justice and religious non-discrimination, is the Imam's encounter with a beggar in Kufa. He made some inquiries about the beggar and was told that he was a Christian who had grown old, become blind and thus incapable of working. The Imam remonstrated with the people in the neighbourhood: 'You have employed him to the point where he is old and infirm, and now you refuse to help him. Give him a regular stipend from the public funds.' We have here the very principle of what in today's lexicon would be called the 'welfare state': the principle that the state has the duty to help those unable to help themselves. This principle is clearly expressed in the following crucial passage of his letter to Malik. It is the only passage which begins with the oath, 'By God, by God!' as if Imam 'Ali wished to underline the absolute importance of what he was about to write:

Then—O God, O God!—[pay particular attention to] the lowest class, those who have no wherewithal, the destitute, the needy, the afflicted, the disabled. Within this class are those who beg, and those whose state of poverty calls out for relief, but they do not beg. Be mindful of God in regard to their rights, for He has entrusted these rights to your care. Assign to them a portion from your public funds, and a portion of the produce of what is taken as booty by the Muslims in every region; for those who are furthest have the same rights as those nearest. Upholding the right of each of them is incumbent upon you. Do not let any haughtiness on your part cause you to neglect them, for you will not be pardoned even the slightest shortcoming [in fulfilling your obligations towards them] as a result of attending to some important matter [deemed to take precedence over your obligations to the poor].

Not only is Malik charged with appointing a kind of 'minister' whose remit is to look after the needy, but also he himself must assume direct responsibility for them:

Apportion a part of your time to those who have special needs, making yourself free to attend to them personally, sitting with them in a public assembly with all due humility before God, your Creator. Keep your soldiers, guards and officers away from them, so that they can speak to you in an uninhibited manner, for I heard the Messenger of God say—God bless him and his family—on more than one occasion: 'A nation in which the rights of the weak are not wrested in an uninhibited manner from the strong will never be blessed.'

We might note here that the Imam ensured that he himself was given no special treatment when he appeared in a court of law as a claimant. A Jew had stolen a shield that belonged to Imam 'Ali. He took the Jew to court even though he had the power, as caliph, simply to reclaim it. Instead, he preferred to uphold the rule of law and willingly submit to due process. The judge in the case, Shurayh, tried to give the Imam a seat of honour, but he told Shurayh to treat him like any ordinary plaintiff: everyone was equal before the law. The case was decided in favour of the Jew, as the Imam could produce no witnesses to support his claim. The Imam accepted the verdict; but the Jew, scarcely able to believe what had happened, confessed that the shield did indeed belong to the Imam. Stunned by the Imam's impeccable virtue—and his respect for the rule of law—he embraced Islam.

Let us mention here Imam 'Ali's attitude to religious minorities. His way of implementing the Islamic institution of *dhimma*, that is, the protection of religious minorities by the Muslim state in return for the payment of a poll-tax (*jizya*), is remarkable. He refers to this principle as follows: 'Those who have contracted the agreement of *dhimma* have done so, such that their lives and their properties should be as inviolable as our own.' He further underscored the legal equality between Muslims and protected minorities by saying that the compensation for the killing of a Christian or Jew was the same as that for a Muslim. He continuously stressed the principle of non-discrimination between Muslims and non-Muslims. For example, it is related in the sources that he distributed a certain amount of state revenue equally to two women, one an Arab, the other a Jew; but the Arab woman complained indignantly: 'I am an Arab and this one is a non-Arab!' The Imam replied: 'By God, I find no grounds for favouring the descendants of Ishmael over those of Isaac.' One is reminded here of Imam 'Ali's supra-confessional, universal view of religion, as expressed in such statements as the following: 'Were the people to set up a chair of judgement for me, I would judge the Muslims in accordance with the Qur'an, the Jews in accordance with the Torah, the people of the Psalms in accordance with the Psalms, the Christians in accordance with the Gospels.'

Returning to his letter to Malik, the Imam describes the temptations of pride, self-aggrandisement and corruption in a way which brings our attention to bear on the spiritual dimensions of these vices, which translate egotism and vanity (or simply: a bad character) into tyrannical oppression:

> Do not say, 'I have been given authority, I order and am obeyed,' for this leads to corruption in the heart and the erosion of religion; and it brings closer the adversities of fate. If the authority of your position engenders vanity and arrogance, then look at the grandeur of God's dominion above you, and at His power to do for you that which you have no power to do for yourself. This will calm your ambition, restrain you from your own vehemence, and bring you back to your senses [literally: bring back to you your intellect which has gone astray]. Beware of comparing yourself with God in greatness and likening yourself to Him in might, for God abases every tyrant and disgraces every braggart. Be just with God and be just with people [giving them what is their due] from yourself, from your close relatives, and from those of your subjects towards whom you are most affectionate. If you fail to do this, you will be an oppressor... Nothing so surely induces the removal of God's grace and hastens His punishment as persistence in oppression. For God hears the cry of the oppressed and keeps a vigilant watch over the oppressors.

One of the ways in which the Imam taught the Muslims to avoid oppression pertains to warfare. All the rules of war established so clearly and definitively by the Prophet (see Ghazi b. Muhammad (ed.), *War and Peace in Islam*, for a comprehensive overview) were upheld by the Imam, who added to them particular precepts, later enshrined in the books of law, pertaining to war between Muslims. As noted earlier, these precepts were imparted by the Imam in accordance with the highest ideals of chivalry and magnanimity. As regards war in the context of inter-imperial rivalry, and the urgent imperative to seek and maintain a state of peace as the final goal in any conflict, the following advice to Malik is worth quoting:

> Never reject any call to peace made to you by your enemy... for truly in peace lies repose for your soldiers, relaxation of your concerns, and security for your lands.... If you and your enemy enter into a solemn agreement, or if he obtain from you the right of protection (*dhimma*), then faithfully abide by what you have promised, and honourably uphold your obligation of protection. Make your very life a shield for what you have promised, for there is no divine obligation which so strongly unites people—despite having diverse inclinations and multifarious opinions—as that of honouring the principle of fulfilling one's pledge. The polytheists had observed this amongst themselves—even apart from their dealings with the Muslims; such was their dread of the consequences of treachery.
>
> So do not violate your pledge of protection, do not break your promises, and do not be treacherous towards your enemy—for only an ignorant wretch (*jahil shaqiyy*) dares to oppose God. God has indeed made His pledge and His protection a means of security, spreading it over His servants by His mercy, a sanctuary in the impregnability of which they find peace, and towards the protective power of which they make haste. So let there be no corruption, no treachery, and no deception. Do not enter into any agreement which contains defects, nor fall back on ambiguous connotations once the agreement has been confirmed and solemnized. Do not let any difficult matter lead you to break unfairly an agreement which God has made binding upon you. For indeed, your patience in the face of a difficulty—hoping for its resolution and its positive outcome—is far better than acting treacherously and then fearing its consequence: being overwhelmed by

an exacting demand from God, from which you will not be able to seek exemption in this life or the next.

Beware of unlawfully shedding blood: nothing is more conducive to retribution, more grave in consequence, more deserving of the cessation of blessings and the severance of one's term [of life] than the unjust shedding of blood. On the Day of Resurrection, God—glorified be He—commences judgement of His servants by [calling them to account over] the blood they have shed. So do not try and strengthen your authority by unlawful bloodshed, for such action in fact weakens and debilitates it, indeed, brings it to an end and removes it.

You have no excuse before God or before me if you intentionally murder anyone, for this calls forth capital punishment. If you fall prey to some error, and your tongue or your hand goes too far in inflicting punishment—for even a punch, and other such assaults, can be a cause of death—do not allow pride in your power to make you seek a way of avoiding payment of what is rightfully due as recompense to the relatives of the person killed.

Finally, let us note the important spiritual advice given to Malik by the Imam. In our times, it appears odd to speak about 'spiritual advice' while formulating a charter of political governance, but Imam 'Ali was perfectly aware that every human institution, however well organised, is only ever going to be as good as the individuals who run it. From the Imam's point of view—the Islamic point of view—pride, hypocrisy and pretentiousness ruin a person's character, and thus undermine the individual's ability to act justly in the discharge of official responsibilities. Moral conscience is inseparable from administrative efficacy; and spiritual consciousness, the depth of faith, is the key source and sustenance of moral conscience. Hence, according to this point of view, the strongest foundation of political justice is that specific kind of incorruptible rectitude which flows from, and is fashioned by, spiritual awareness: it is one's knowledge of the Truth (*al-Haqq*), which spontaneously and effortlessly generates appropriate action for the sake of the right (*al-haqq*) of each and every person in society, and which renders the individual official immune to the temptations offered by political power:

> Beware of being self-satisfied, of being over-confident in what you find impressive about yourself, and of loving to be flattered, for these are among Satan's most reliable opportunities to efface the virtue (*ihsan*) of the virtuous (*muhsinin*). Beware of making your subjects beholden to you for your benevolence towards them; of exaggerating your deeds; and of making promises to them which you break. For making people beholden ruins virtue; exaggeration removes the light of the truth; and breaking promises imposes upon you the hatred of God and men. God the Exalted has said: 'It is indeed hateful to God that ye say that which ye do not' (Q 61:3)... Soon, the veil covering all affairs will be lifted for you, and justice will be sought from you by those who have been wronged.

One must therefore master oneself, this being an essential prerequisite for ruling over others. But, in the Imam's perspective, self-mastery is impossible without the grace of God; this grace is ever present, but due to our forgetfulness (*ghafla*) of God, we lack receptivity to it. What is most urgently needed for self-mastery, then, is the remembrance of God. The relationship between mastery of oneself and the remembrance of God is made particularly clear in this passage:

> Dominate the zeal of your pride, the vehemence of your castigation, the power of your hand, and the sharpness of your tongue. Guard against these vices by restraining all impulsiveness, and putting off all resort to force until your anger subsides and you regain self-control. But you

cannot attain such self-domination without increasing your pre-occupation with remembrance of your return to your Lord.

This is why, despite the many tasks the governor has to perform, the most important is what brings him closer to God: 'Give to God your vital energy in your nights and your days, and perform fully that by which you draw near to Him, doing so perfectly, without becoming dull or deficient, taking your body to its limits.' We mentioned in the Introduction that Imam 'Ali is known in the Islamic tradition as an exemplar of the complete or perfect human being, *al-insan al-kamil*. In the above passage, this complete human being reminds us that every dimension of our lives must be integrated into the whole, tightly woven into a unity which participates in the substance of *tawhid*, 'making one'. Even if Malik—and by extension any ruler or holder of office—is going to be governing a province, his principal concern must be spiritual and not political. Or rather, to follow the logic of the Imam's ethos, at once spiritual, moral and, if it be one's God-given duty, political: the governor's political actions will be just if he has moral integrity, and his integrity will be consolidated in the measure of his spirituality. This spirituality implies that there must be no desire to rule; as the Prophet said to a man who asked to be governor of Yemen: 'Your desire to rule disqualifies you.' The governor is one who rules because he has been asked to rule by the caliph; and the caliph, Imam 'Ali, rules, as we have seen above, not because he wishes to—his detachment from the world dissolves all such desire—but because it was incumbent upon him as the person most qualified to rule. 'Stay away from [political] power' (*taba'id min al-sultan*), the Imam advises us, and links this aversion to politics (using his customary rhyming prose) to the avoidance of complacency in the face of the 'deceptions of the devil' (*khuda' al-shaytan*) (Qutbuddin, *Treasury*, 77).

The governor, then, must spend as much time as he can,

each night, in prayer, meditation and remembrance, taking his body to its limits in worship, even if on the morrow he has to run the affairs of state (but, it should be noted, he must not become 'dull or deficient' as a result of lack of sleep). One observes here the dynamic of *tawhid* working on all planes, leading to spiritual and ethical well-being for the individual, and to political and social justice for the collectivity. In his recommendation to Malik to pray long hours each night, Imam 'Ali is again describing himself, or rather his own way of life, which was at one with that of the Prophet. Even in the Medina period, as head of state, the Prophet is told by God in the Qur'an: 'Truly your Lord knows that you stand in prayer close to two-thirds of the night, and [sometimes] half of the night, and [sometimes] a third of the night—you and a group of those with you' (73:20). Imam 'Ali was in the forefront of this 'group' (*ta'ifa*). Together, these heroes of nascent Islam were making history by day, while engaging in intense worship by night. Human history was being made by those whose souls were immersed in divine mystery. As Imam 'Ali asks God in his most famous supplication, *Du'a' Kumayl*: 'Make all my time, in the night and the day, inhabited by Your remembrance.' This is because the perpetual remembrance of God, *dhikr Allah*, is the cure for all ailments of the soul. As he also says in this supplication: 'O He whose Name is a remedy and whose invocation (*dhikr*) is the cure.'

◆

To conclude these reflections on the caliphate of Imam 'Ali, let us return to the prophecy of the Prophet, that 'Ali would fight for the *ta'wil* of the Qur'an as he, the Prophet had had to fight for its *tanzil*. It is significant that the Prophet used the word 'fight' in his prophecy about 'Ali's mission to teach the meaning of *ta'wil*. He also accurately prophesied that 'Ali would fight three groups of people: the oath-breakers (*al-nakithun*), the deviators (*al-qasitun*), and the renegades (*al-mariqun*). Is there a connection between these two prophecies?

We think so. To begin with, it is significant that the way in which the Prophet imparts the first prophecy is through an allusion, *ishara*. As just noted, 'Ali's name is not mentioned in the prophecy about who would fight for *ta'wil*: instead he mentions 'the one who is mending my sandals.' It is possible, therefore, that we are being asked to interpret Imam 'Ali's battles spiritually, according to the method of *ta'wil*, and thus to see them as possible allusions to mystical challenges and confrontations within the soul. In the spirit of *ta'wil* evoked in Chapter 1, we can see a correspondence between the outer battles of the Imam and the inner battles of the soul, the 'greatest' *jihad*, briefly alluded to in the previous chapter ('Abd al-Razzaq Kashani has given us, in his commentary cited earlier, a systematic application of this mode of *ta'wil* to the Qur'an: it is designated as *tatbiq*, 'the establishing of correspondence' between the inner and the outer worlds).

As we have seen earlier, Imam 'Ali alludes to the multitude of forces within the soul that need to be 'fought', overcome, and won over to the side of the Truth. If the whole universe is encapsulated within a single human soul, the soul that is also 'The Clear Book', then the converse is also true: the outer, physical battles fought in the world can be interpreted, symbolically and microcosmically, as 'greater' spiritual battles within that 'small cosmos' that the soul constitutes. Imam Ja'far al-Sadiq, as if commenting upon his ancestor's saying about the confrontation between the 'forces' of egotistic desire and those of the intellect, refers to seventy-five 'armies' (*junud*) in the soul, commanded by the intellect, who oppose seventy-five armies in the soul, commanded by ignorance. The armies of the intellect consist of all the fundamental virtues and spiritual qualities, while those of ignorance are composed of all the vices and defects of the soul.

In this light, it is possible to see how the three adversaries whom Imam 'Ali had to fight outwardly on the field of battle can symbolize forces within the soul which must be overcome, if the intellect is to achieve victory against *al-Shaytan*, on behalf of *al-Rahman*. Let us remember that each of his three sets of adversaries was formally Muslim; this is in stark contrast to the battles waged by the Prophet, who only fought in self-defence against those opposed to the formal and literal Message, the *zahir* of the message. The Prophet was, literally, 'fighting' for the *tanzil* of the Islamic Revelation against those who overtly disbelieved in it and raged against it; Imam 'Ali, by contrast, was fighting against Muslims, those who formally accepted the letter of the Revelation, but were nonetheless violating different aspects of its spirit and declaring war on him: not only the legitimate ruler of the Muslims, but also the very personification of the spirit of the Revelation.

This spiritual interiorization of the battles seems to 'work' clearly in the case of Imam 'Ali's second and third opponents, the 'deviators' and the 'renegades': on the one hand, Mu'awiya and his cohorts were the epitome of hypocritical worldliness hiding behind a transparent façade of religious rectitude; on the other, the Kharijites exemplified blind fanaticism in the guise of intense piety. But it is not so easy to see how the actions of such great companions as Talha and Zubayr, not to mention the wife of the Prophet, 'Aisha, can be interpreted according to this *ta'wil*, even if both Talha and Zubayr were indeed in the category of the *nakithun*, the 'oath-breakers', having broken their oath of allegiance to Imam 'Ali—an oath which they claimed later was taken under duress. Imam 'Ali helps us to see how we can 'read' their opposition to him according to the spirit of *ta'wil*.

First, in his citation of verse 15:47 (as noted above), whereby he hopes that all bitterness be taken from the breasts of Talha and Zubayr, so that they enter Paradise with him as brothers. Here we see that even virtuous souls, destined for Paradise, can nonetheless suffer a terrible fall on earth. Second,

121

in microcosmic terms, Imam 'Ali teaches us that even great virtues within the soul can lead to a fall in the spiritual life, unless the soul as a whole be penetrated by humility, the prelude to self-effacement which itself is the threshold of victory in the spiritual quest. The Imam teaches this subtle truth in many sayings. For example: 'The sin that gives you grief is better, in the sight of God, than the virtue that makes you proud.' Talha, Zubayr and 'Aisha, then, can symbolize the virtues in the soul that, instead of fighting on the side of the intellect—personified to perfection by Imam 'Ali—are hijacked by the adversary, and then duped into fighting instead on the side of the ego, whose desire, *hawa*, is taken as an implicit 'god'. The Qur'an asks us rhetorically 'Have you seen the one who takes his *hawa* as his god?' (25:43; repeated at 45:23) The implication here is of a covert idolatry, *al-shirk al-khafi*, referred to by the Prophet as the most difficult sin of all to detect in the soul.

This inner idolatry accompanies, but inwardly poisons, the formal affirmation of faith in God. 'Most of them do not believe in God,' says the Qur'an, 'without being idolaters' (12:106). The implication here again is that of hidden *shirk*, a trap into which even 'the believers' can fall—the majority of them, in fact, according to this verse. The mystical literature of the world's religious traditions is filled with instances of the cunning ways in which the hidden idolatry of the ego enables pride and pretension to subvert faithful and virtuous souls. It is not for nothing that the Prophet referred to this inner battle as being *akbar*; it is not only 'greater' but infinitely more subtle, and thus immeasurably more difficult to fight than any outer battle.

However, the entry of Talha and Zubayr into Paradise can signify, as can 'Aisha's repentance, the transformative grace of *al-Rahman*, bringing to the right side of the soul these virtues which are good in substance, but which nonetheless contributed to pride in the soul, thus opening the way to a fall. They are redeemed by the mercy of God, but only after their rebellion against the intellect—symbolised by Imam 'Ali—is overcome. The mercy of God is then expressed by the intellect, Imam 'Ali, praying that all bitterness be removed from their hearts upon their entrance into Paradise. Here, the Imam can be seen to manifest and symbolise the perfect union between knowledge and love, between intelligence and mercy: 'The one who truly understands among all those who understand,' he proclaims, 'is the one who never makes people despair of the mercy of God.' So, in terms of the violation of the oath of allegiance made by Talha and Zubayr to Imam 'Ali—making them, as just noted, the *nakithun*, or 'oath-breakers' prophesied by the Prophet—we might venture the following interpretation. Even sincere and well-intentioned souls who have violated the mystical oath of allegiance (the same term, *bay'a* is used for both types of allegiance) to a spiritual master (*mawla*), those whose virtues contributed to pride and self-aggrandisement instead of humility and self-effacement—even such souls must never despair of the mercy of God. For the simple reason that the worst of sinners—even those guilty of murder, adultery or idolatry—are forgiven by God if their repentance is sincere and they do not repeat their sins. After mentioning those who have committed these three deadly sins, the Qur'an tells us that they will suffer a terrible penalty 'except him who repents and believes, and acts virtuously: those are the ones whose evil acts are changed into beautiful ones. God is ever Forgiving, Merciful' (25:70). Most appropriately, this message of mercy, instilling hope and dispelling despair, comes in the middle of a long, beautiful passage describing the 'slaves of the All-Merciful' (*'ibad al-Rahman*).

◆

In the following chapter we shall examine the way in which Imam 'Ali discharged his responsibilities as spiritual guide and religious teacher, even while burdened with the immense task of governing the state as caliph, and carrying out the grim duty of leading his army as commander-in-chief in three civil wars.

4

The 'Commander of the Faithful' as Spiritual Guide

We saw in the previous chapter that Imam 'Ali's 'political' instruction to Malik al-Ashtar, contrary to what might have been expected, contained a great deal of 'spiritual' guidance. It is important to remember that the Imam continued to act as a spiritual guide even while facing the formidable challenges of governing an empire plunged into civil strife. One might have thought that the exercise of his strictly spiritual role was restricted to the twenty-five year period preceding his accession to the caliphate, but this is far from the truth. Even as caliph, he never ceased to impart spiritual advice and guidance to the community, speaking to each person 'according to the level of his intellect,' in the words of a key prophetic teaching.

It was not simply a question of revealing the deeper truths to those disciples deemed qualified to receive them, while restricting his public teachings to simple principles. For what is perhaps most remarkable about the teachings imparted during his caliphate is the way in which his public sermons (over two hundred of which can be read today in the *Nahj al-balagha*) spoke to all people, fulfilling their ethical and religious needs, while at the same time containing subtle esoteric truths which nourished the aspirations of the mystically inclined minority. A key feature of his dialectic was to inseminate mystical implications within basic ethical teachings, delivered with unsurpassable eloquence, whilst also making subtle allusions to themes expressed or implied in the Qur'an and in prophetic sayings. Teachings on such simple precepts as kindness, generosity, contentment, patience, courage, compassion, self-restraint, detachment, altruism, service, etc.—were replete with openings to higher spiritual truths. Conversely, even in his more esoteric discourses, subtle mystical principles were often taught in a way which allowed their transformative ethical implications to percolate throughout society, rendering them accessible to the consciousness of the simple, pious believer.

Loving Mercy in the *Du'a' Kumayl*

This is not the place for entering into a comprehensive analysis of this mode of teaching, but let us try to see how it appears to have operated in relation to his teaching of one key ethical principle, that of *rahma*, which, as noted in Chapter 1, we should translate as 'loving mercy and compassion'; for the notion of *rahma* is inextricably bound up with the idea of maternal love, and it cannot be restricted to mercy and compassion alone. *Rahma* is one of the central principles which, in Imam 'Ali's discourses, brought together esoteric guidance for the few with exoteric teachings for the many. For it is a principle which encompasses both the highest aspects of divine reality and the most practical imperatives of everyday life. What follows is our attempt to imagine how his teaching on this theme would have been received, how the allusions he makes might have been understood, how the revealed context of his teachings—the Qur'an and the Sunna—would have been constantly alerting his listeners to the deeper implications and ramifications of his discourses.

As discussed in our *Justice and Remembrance* (141-146), one clear example of his allusive mode of teaching is in Sermon 213 of the *Nahj al-balagha*. The Imam first quotes words from verse 37 of Chapter 24, *al-Nur* ('The Light'), in which the invocation of God's Name is mentioned, and then proceeds to comment on them. The words in question are: '... men whom neither trade nor merchandise diverts from the remembrance of God.' The Imam does not mention at all the fact that this part of verse 37 only delivers its full meaning in the context of the preceding verses 35 and 36. Verse 35 is the famous 'verse of light'—*ayat al-nur*—one of the most profound and oft-meditated verses of the whole Qur'an, brimming with mystical symbolism. The Imam did not need to quote the verse, as he knew that his recitation of the words from verse 37 would evoke the preceding verses in the minds of most, if not all, of the listeners. We must note carefully this mode of teaching, rich in ellipsis, hints, allusions and implications, if we wish to discern, infer or intuit what is unsaid from what is said in the Imam's teachings.

One of the most influential and popular of Imam 'Ali's teachings is the supplication, cited above, known as *Du'a' Kumayl*, which is still being recited by millions of Muslims every Thursday night in mosques throughout the world. It is known by this name because the Imam taught the supplication to Kumayl in private, referring to it, in fact, as the supplication of al-Khidr, which Imam 'Ali had received through the inspiration of al-Khidr. Imam 'Ali often referred to al-Khidr (some authorities in the tradition regard him as a prophet, others as a saint) as 'my brother', and claimed that al-Khidr came to him assuming the form of different people (see our discussion of the *'Alawi* archetype in Chapter 1).

In this supplication, the loftiest truths of the transcendent Spirit are interspersed with the deepest yearnings of the repentant soul: the soul, painfully aware of its sinfulness, pleading for the mercy of its Lord. It thus has teachings which are relevant to the whole spectrum of spiritual types, from saints to sinners. Its very first verse establishes the primacy of divine mercy: 'O God, I ask You by Your Mercy "which embraces all things"' (citing Q 7:156; our citations are from the translation by William Chittick, with minor modifications). A few verses further into the supplication, we read: 'by Your Names, which have filled the foundations of all things.' If we put together these two verses, we see an *ishara*, an esoteric allusion which would doubtless be grasped by the spiritually receptive. The Qur'anic idea of divine mercy 'encompassing all things' would alert sensitive listeners to the deeper messages being taught in the supplication. One of these deeper messages is that the essential, defining quality of all of the divine Names, taken together, is *rahma*, for the Qur'an instructs us: 'Call upon Allah or call upon *al-Rahman*,' and continues, 'whichever Name you call upon, unto Him belong all the most beautiful Names' (17:110).

The Name 'al-Rahman' is thus synonymous with 'Allah' (the name 'Allah' simply means 'the Divinity'); it is the Name which most fully reveals the fundamental nature of God: all of the Names 'belong' to al-Rahman, just as they all 'belong' to Allah. To say, then, that the most beautiful divine Names fill the foundations of all things is to say that it is essentially *rahma* that fills the foundation of all things. All the qualities that can be called 'most beautiful', *husna*, are contained in God, of course, but this teaching helps us to see that the essential nature or quality of the Divinity is more fully disclosed by the Name *al-Rahman* than by any other name. This implies that anything which is contrary to loving mercy is only an appearance, not a reality: it has no 'foundation' in Being, because the foundation of Being is nothing other than God's Names, all of which are expressions of the loving mercy—the 'beauty', *al-husn*—of the Absolute. So, whatever is contrary to mercy is ontologically 'unfounded'; that is, it does not really, fully, or permanently, exist; it is only a transient appearance.

The life of this world is compared to a dream in relation to the next world, which is akin to awakening to reality:

'All people are asleep,' said the Imam; 'when they die, they wake up' (this saying is often attributed to the Prophet, but according to scholars of *hadith*, it was uttered by Imam 'Ali). The life of this world can also be described as a mirage, as in the following Qur'anic analogy: 'The thirsty one supposes it to be water till he comes unto it and finds it nothing; and finds instead God...' (24:39). Or again: 'The life of this world is but distraction and play; and the abode of the Hereafter—that is true Life, if only they knew' (29:64).

So, one might paraphrase the first *shahada*, 'no divinity but God,' by saying: there is no reality other than mercy. Or, as the Qur'an tells us: *la ilaha illa Huwa'r-Rahman ar-Rahim* (2:163), which we can translate as follows: 'no divinity but Him [who is, by nature], the lovingly Compassionate, the lovingly Merciful.' We could also paraphrase *Huwa'r-Rahman ar-Rahim* as 'He who creates all beings through compassionate love, and who saves all beings through loving mercy.' Again, we see that Imam 'Ali's inspired teaching implies and branches out into the infinitely expandable realm of divine Revelation; to understand the implications of the all-embracing nature of *rahma*, one would need to meditate on all the instances in the Qur'an where this theme is mentioned or implied. As Imam 'Ali said, and as discussed in Chapter 1, 'Parts of the Qur'an speak through other parts, and some parts of it bear witness to other parts.'

One such 'part' where the theme of *rahma* figures prominently is in the narrative concerning al-Khidr. The supplication attributed by Imam 'Ali to the inspiration of al-Khidr is indeed pregnant with allusions to the polyvalent teachings taught by al-Khidr in the Surat al-Kahf ('The Cave'; no. 18), one of the most esoterically fertile chapters of the Qur'an (again, as noted in Chapter 1). One aspect of the narrative to which we should pay particular attention is the way in which all three lessons imparted by al-Khidr to Moses are bound up with divine mercy: al-Khidr partly damages the boat of poor people, only to pre-

vent a tyrannical king from expropriating it; he kills a youth
only because he knew that the youth would inflict evil upon his
parents, and that God would give the parents a righteous and
'more merciful' son in his stead; and al-Khidr rebuilds a crum-
bling wall to protect a treasure that was the property of two
orphans, thus enabling them to inherit their rightful legacy—
all of this being done 'as a mercy from your Lord' (18:79–82).

The principle of mercy which dominates the *Duʿaʾ Kumayl*
thus resonates with the Qurʾanic teaching of al-Khidr. One of
the simple, practical lessons that all people can derive from the
supplication, in the light of the Qurʾanic narrative concerning
al-Khidr, is this: however baffling or absurd be the events by
which one is confronted in this world, there is a hidden mercy
which the ordinary person only comes to perceive when the
veil of this world is lifted at death. For the sages and saints,
however, this all-embracing divine mercy is seen already, while
they are alive, as the *benevolent reality* penetrating all things,
the *loving creativity* from which all things originally came, and
that *merciful finality* to which they ultimately return. For they,
like Imam ʿAli, can see through the veil of this world even while
living within it. As noted earlier, he said: 'Were the veil [of this
world] to be removed, I could not be increased in certainty.'
And again: 'The day has dawned [already] for those with eyes
to see.' Imam ʿAli always sees the dawning of the divine Light
with the eye of his heart, despite the fact that the five years
of his turbulent caliphate saw little other than dark storm
clouds obscuring the light of the sun, to use the terms of his
metaphor.

The vision in question here is that of the absolute goodness
and mercy of God. Imam ʿAli 'sees' this with his heart, which
means that the knowledge of God attained through this vision
permeates his entire being: the absolute goodness of God
is not just apprehended in an intellectual sense; rather, it
is 'tasted' in an experiential sense. Indeed, the saints are
spiritually drunk on the wine of contemplation, but their

inward inebriation goes hand in hand with outward sobriety. It is the bliss given to them inwardly, by their vision of divine Beauty, that is their most powerful 'theodicy'. In other words, it is the means by which the infinite goodness and absolute power of God are upheld, despite the existence of evil, suffering and absurdity in the world. The thorny problems generated by reason in the face of these negative phenomena are resolved for the saints existentially and spiritually, rather than just logically or philosophically: the long hours they stand in meditative prayer, reciting Scripture, invoking God's Name—doing so each and every night—is not so much 'food for thought' as nourishment for the heart. Their worship nourishes and deepens their spiritual intuition of ultimate Reality, the *Haqiqa*. Such intimate and blissful contact with the absolute goodness of God transforms the minds of these saints in a way scarcely imaginable to those who pray only mechanically, let alone those who do not pray at all.

The prayers, supplications, incantations, meditations and invocations of the Ahl al-Bayt come forth from gratitude, Imam 'Ali assures us: gratitude for what has already been given to them by God. Those who worship thus are called by him 'the liberated ones' (*al-ahrar*), in contrast to those who worship out of fear ('the slaves') and those who worship out of desire ('the merchants'). The Prophet, when asked by one of his wives why he was praying all night, such that his feet became swollen, replied: 'Am I not a grateful servant?' Such liberated souls worship God with gratitude for what He has given them here in this world: what they have received is a heartfelt 'taste', not just conceptual knowledge, of the absolute, unimpeachable goodness—the pure *rahma*— of ultimate Reality, and of Paradise, which is the radiance of that goodness. It is this spiritual vision that explains how Imam 'Ali was able to claim that his heart was already in Paradise, even amid the appalling tribulations he had to endure on earth. Likewise, it is this that explains how his

131

daughter, Zaynab, could say, regarding the horrific slaughter of her brother, Imam Husayn, and his 72 companions at Karbala: 'I saw nothing but beauty' (*ma ra'aytu illa jamilan*). All earthly suffering is reduced to illusion before the vision of the beatitude of true Reality, *al-Haqiqa*.

This is not to say that Imam 'Ali and the Ahl al-Bayt were fatalists, passively accepting all things, seeing only the beauty and goodness of God in everything, including tyranny and injustice. Evil remains evil; but the level of existence on which evil exists is eclipsed by the perpetually dawning light of absolute goodness, which they see with the heart; that is, with a spiritual intuition surpassing ordinary modes of perception and cognition. It is this vision of the heart that enables them to inwardly transcend the realm of outward phenomena. One might object: how can this exalted degree of spiritual vision enjoyed by the Ahl al-Bayt help ordinary believers, struggling to make sense of the absurdities and sufferings in their lives?

One answer is that merely hearing the words of the Ahl al-Bayt describing their vision, and seeing how they overcame, inwardly, all manner of trial and suffering, serves to deepen or awaken an already existing sense of the infinite reality and the inexplicable intimacy of divine mercy. For the core of each person's heart is made up of the creative projection of divine *rahma*: 'Al-Rahman... created man' (55:1,3). It is from this intrinsically merciful substance of the heart that there arises not only faith in God, but also unshakeable trust (*tawakkul*) in His mercy, together with serene submission to His will—however adverse be the outward circumstances of life. Ordinary Muslims need only look at the dignified way in which the Ahl al-Bayt confronted and overcame trial after trial, disaster after disaster, to have their faith reinforced, to take heart, and to help them overcome the trials of their own life.

As we saw in Chapter 1, the Prophet said: 'The believers are well in all circumstances.' In the face of evil, suffering and tribulation, the believers may not be able to untangle the complex webs of causality such as to arrive at a philosophically neat theodicy; but through faith and patience, courage and contentment, trust and submission, they are able to endure all tribulations, knowing that mercy will have the last word. Meanwhile, they struggle against injustice, but their outward struggle is accompanied by an inward composure, for they know, viscerally, that the outcome of their effort is entirely in the hands of God. Their duty is to do what they can with a pure and good intention, knowing that 'acts are judged according to their intentions,' as the Prophet said, and that consequently their reward is already given in the very fact that they are sincerely striving for virtue: 'Is the reward of virtue anything other than virtue?' asks the Qur'an (55:60).

The sincere quest for virtue, however, is not motivated by desire for any reward from God for oneself. On the contrary, the quest for virtue is sincere in the measure that it is motivated by a desire to give oneself to God. As noted earlier, the 'most pious' (al-atqa), according to the Qur'an, is he who acts in a perfectly generous and charitable way, but for no reward 'other than desire for the Face of His Lord Most High'; such a person, the Qur'an assures us, 'will be content' (92:20–21). One might add: *only* such a person will be content, for any attachment to reward for oneself in this world will inevitably result in suffering. We have in this Qur'anic message, a lesson in the Hindu doctrine of *nishkama karma* ('action without desire'), as taught in the Bhagavad Gita (4:14 *et passim*): one acts without desire for the fruits of one's actions in this world. One does one's duty as well as one can, for the sake of God, and expecting nothing for oneself in this world, knowing that such expectation will inevitably end in disappointment, if not misery and suffering. 'My far-fetched hopes have held me back from my true gain,' the sinner confesses, in the *Du'a' Kumayl*. Imam 'Ali warns us: ' Your resolve to do good deeds will be weakened by false hope,' adding: 'if you were to empty your heart of false hope, it would urge you once again to perform good deeds.' In similar vein: 'Most shattered minds have been felled by lightning bolts of covetous desires' (Qutbuddin, *Treasury*, 55, 231).

Returning to the 'most pious' (or 'most God-conscious'), *al-atqa*, the one most possessed of *taqwa*, Imam 'Ali tells us that the most significant thing about our actions is, precisely, our God-consciousness, our *taqwa*. This term denotes the entire spectrum of pious attitudes, from scrupulous fear of God to permanent loving consciousness of God. If action is motivated by *taqwa*, then it is, by definition, acceptable to God: 'Action with *taqwa* is never insignificant; for how can that which is accepted by God ever be deemed insignificant?' the Imam asks us rhetorically. The Qur'an is replete with references to *taqwa*. In the context of the present discussion—how to overcome the calamities and afflictions of life—the following passage is important. It helps us to appreciate the implication of Imam 'Ali's statement about acts being 'accepted' by God:

> Whoever is piously conscious of God, for him God will establish a way out (*makhraj*), and will provide for him in a manner beyond his expectations; and whoever puts his trust in God, God will suffice him. God attains his purpose. Indeed, God has appointed for everything a measure (65:2–3).

One might object here: but God did not always establish a 'way out' of the tribulations suffered by Imam 'Ali—he had to suffer disaster after disaster, culminating in his tragic death at the hands of an assassin. One answer we can give is this: Imam 'Ali was *always* given a way out of his tribulations, but it was not necessarily of the outward, phenomenal order: his permanent 'way out' of all afflictions was of a spiritual, inward order. As we saw in Chapter 1, in the very moment when he was mortally wounded, his reflex reaction was to embrace his death as a triumphant liberation. For his permanent *taqwa*, his perpetual consciousness of God—together with his absolute trust in God and submission to divinely ordained destiny, as mentioned in the Qur'anic passage just cited—these spiritual attitudes gave him access to the *inward* path of liberation, a path which is perpetually present and available to each and every person whose heart has been enlivened by faith.

Being inwardly or spiritually liberated from the world means always having access to a 'way out' of the potentially crippling intensity of whatever trials one might be facing in the world. This does not mean that outer difficulties will not affect us at all; it just means that they cannot affect the core of our being. The soul may feel some degree of stress and strain, concern and worry, but the heart will not suffer anxiety, still less depression or despair. The Imam advises us to rid ourselves of 'the fevers of anxiety' with patient fortitude and beautiful certitude; to cut ourselves off from the 'roots of anxiety' with the power of patience; to shed tears during our supplications to God at dawn, for they 'douse the sea of fire engulfing the supplicant' (Qutbuddin, *Treasury*, 79-81). He teaches us how to divest ourselves of debilitating and depressing anxiety through maintaining a prudent and wise balance in our states of happiness and unhappiness in this world, on the one hand; and through being more concerned about our state of soul in the Hereafter, on the other. Proper concern with our eternal abode will eradicate all disproportionate anxieties connected with our life in this transient world:

> If something of this world comes to you from God, do not exult excessively. If He keeps something from you, do not grieve excessively. Save your worries for what comes after death (Qutbuddin, *Treasury*, 107; translation modified).

This saying takes us back to the theme of *zuhd*, which we discussed earlier. Imam 'Ali, in one of the aphorisms of the *Nahj*, tells us that the meaning of *zuhd* is contained in the following two injunctions of the Qur'an: on the one hand, 'do not despair over what has passed you by'; on the other, 'do not exult over what He has given you' (57:23). One despairs over deprivation in this world only if this world is the focus of one's aspirations; if, by contrast, one's aspirations are firmly focused on the Hereafter, then no amount of deprivation in this world can cause despair. The complementary teaching is equally liberating: if one restrains one's tendency to exaggerate the importance of comforts in this world, and avoids exultation over such worldly well-being, then one eliminates (or at least reduces) one's susceptibility to despair and depression when the inevitable befalls: the removal of that well-being—either in this life, through unforeseeable adversity, or at death, the unavoidable finality.

To prevent oneself from falling into the double pitfall of despair and exultation requires a high degree of detachment from what is both disagreeable and agreeable in this world; and this detachment is possible only if one's focus is fundamentally otherworldly. In the light of the evil of hell and the bliss of Paradise, all possible woes and joys on earth are rendered insignificant. As Imam 'Ali says, in another aphorism from the *Nahj*: 'There is no goodness in a good thing if it is followed by the Fire; and there is no evil in an evil thing if it is followed by the Garden. Every benefit apart from the Garden is negligible; and every tribulation apart from the Fire is well-being' (*'afiya*). The reality of a thing is only to be discovered in its consequence, in how it ends, where it leads. One must see each phenomenon in this world as a seed which will come to fruition in the next world; a seed either of celestial felicity or infernal misery. As we saw above, the Imam tells us that we are all asleep in this world, and we wake up only in the next one. But even though he knew that this life is only a dream compared to the Hereafter, he insisted that one must take this 'dream' with the utmost seriousness, on its own level of reality. To quote one of his best known sayings: 'Work for this world as if you were to live forever, and work for the Hereafter as if you were to die tomorrow.'

One senses in such inspirational teachings the reason why the Prophet compared his Ahl al-Bayt to Noah's Ark: 'Whoever enters it is saved, and whoever turns away from it perishes.' One might again object and ask: what kind of safety was given to Imam 'Ali's son, the grandson of the Prophet, Imam Husayn, and the members of the Ahl al-Bayt, at Karbala? One way of answering this question is to return to the meaning of *zuhd*: it is to deem this world, and all it contains, of little significance, and to understand that, in the words of the Qur'an, cited above, 'the abode of the Hereafter—that is true Life, if only they knew' (29:64). Salvation is entering Paradise in the Hereafter; and, in this world, it is all that contributes to that outcome. So, being safe in this world does not mean being spared all trials and afflictions; it means being granted the capacity to endure all trials and afflictions. In other words, we are 'saved' in this world if, when we are hit by the stormy waves of calamity and tribulation, we embark upon the saving ark of *zuhd*, together with all the fundamental spiritual attitudes preached and practised by the Prophet and his Ahl al-Bayt. We are thereby shielded against the tidal waves of anxiety, misery and terror, with which the calamities of the world are trying to engulf and drown us. 'Anguish makes a calamity complete,' Imam 'Ali said (Qutbuddin, *Treasury*, 225; translation modified). The implication is that, if we can prevent our soul from falling into anguish when hit by a calamity, the calamity will not be 'complete': the storm waves may rock and buffet the boat we are in, but the boat will not capsize.

According to the Qur'an, we shall be tried in this world with 'something of fear, hunger, loss of wealth, souls [of loved ones] and fruits [of your labour]'; but it immediately adds: 'give good news to the patient, those who, when afflicted with calamity, say, "Truly, we belong to God, and verily unto Him we are returning." They are the ones upon whom are blessings and mercy from their Lord, and they are the rightly guided' (2:155-157). Here, patience is given as the key quality implying all the spiritual attitudes that flow from awareness of God as both Creator and Saviour—as *al-Rahman* and *al-Rahim*. There is no space in the soul of the patient and trusting believer in God for that 'anguish' which, in the saying of Imam 'Ali just cited, 'makes a calamity complete.'

We may well be afflicted by a worldly calamity—even if it be but once: when the whole world collapses for us in a single moment, as it does when we die; but if we respond to worldly calamity with patience fortified by faith, rather than anguish spiralling into terror, then that calamity can only remain partial or peripheral: it will affect only our outer self, not our inner core. We know, viscerally and subliminally, that God is pure *rahma*, so we never 'blame God' for our trials and tribulations, even if we know that nothing happens but by the will of God. Our consciousness of the absolute goodness of God is derived from heartfelt certainty, not fallible conjecture; so in our heart of hearts we know that, however baffled our minds might be by the cause of our afflictions, our submission to God's will produces a state of peace in the soul which prevails over the potentially unsettling questions in our minds. To the extent that our submission is complete, our sense of insecurity will dissolve; and we will be granted composure and peace in proportion to the depth of our faith—what St Paul refers to as 'the peace of God that transcends all understanding' (Philippians, 4:7).

The Prophet said: 'This world is cursed, and all that it contains is cursed, except the remembrance of God.' The 'curse' with which all things in the world are afflicted is the touch of death; so, if we are detached from that which dies, and instead attach ourselves to the remembrance of That which is eternal, the result is entering the salvific Ark—the safety of the remembrance of God, conditioned by the quality of *zuhd*, which dissolves the roots of anguish, terror and anxiety from our souls. *Zuhd* carries us, here and now, into that spiritual security and inner serenity which the remembrance of God, alone, engenders: 'Is it not in the remembrance of God that hearts are at peace?' (Q 13:28).

What is Reality?

Returning to the theme of *rahma*: in what is called the *Hadith al-Haqiqa* ('Saying concerning ultimate Reality'), another famous dialogue between Imam 'Ali and Kumayl, the beauty of reality is powerfully reinforced.

Kumayl asks: 'What is reality (*ma al-Haqiqa*)?'

'What have you got to do with Reality?' the Imam replies.

'Am I not the companion of your secret (*sahib sirrik*)?' asks Kumayl.

'Yes,' says the Imam, 'but what drips upon you gushes from me.'

The Imam then gives five statements, after each one of which Kumayl asks for further clarification:

1. *Al-haqiqa* is the unveiling of the splendours of Majesty, without any allusion.

2. The effacement of that which is erroneously imagined, together with the clarity of that which is truly known (*mahw al-mawhum wa-sahw al-ma'lum*).

3. The rending of the veil through the triumph of the mystery.

4. The attraction of absolute unity to the quality of unification (*jadhb al-ahadiyya li-sifat al-tawhid*).

5. A light dawning from the morn of eternity, its traces shimmering on the temples of *tawhid*.

After this statement, when Kumayl asks for more clarification, the Imam says: 'Extinguish the lamp, morning has broken!' We have here an astonishing set of evocative images, reminding us of the koans of Zen Buddhism. Many commentaries have been written on this extraordinary discourse. The key principle which the commentators have focused on is that of divine Self-disclosure, *tajalli*. The ultimate Reality is the divine Essence, by whose acts of Self-disclosure the entire cosmos is brought into being. God manifests His Light as majestic radiance, the traces of this light falling upon what the Imam calls the 'temples of *tawhid*'. As the word *haykal* (pl. *hayakil*), can be translated as 'body', we can interpret these temples as all of the creatures in the cosmos. God's Self-manifestation is thus identical not only with the creation of all things, but also with the creation of those things as 'temples of *tawhid*': each created thing can thus be seen as a sacred precinct within which the spiritual activity of *tawhid* takes place. If we recall that *tawhid* essentially means 'declaring/affirming/realising oneness,' we see that it is a dynamic spiritual process, not a static mental concept; in other words, it is the quintessence, or the deepest substance, of prayer.

'The attraction of absolute unity to the quality of unification.' We see, with the help of the principle highlighted in the *Du'a' Kumayl*—no reality apart from mercy—that this attraction is nothing other than the magnetic power of *rahma*. It is God's loving mercy, as al-Rahim, which exerts a merciful, saving attraction upon all beings; upon all those beings who have been created as a result of God's loving compassion, al-Rahman. We have a vision here of *rahma* coming full circle: the circle of divine Self-disclosure begins with creative *rahma*, and is completed by saving *rahma*; al-Rahman projects and creates all beings, al-Rahim attracts and reintegrates all beings. This re-integration is, precisely, *tawhid*, a process of 'making one', unifying that which appears to be multiple. It is a process which shows us that what Imam 'Ali calls 'the light dawning from the morn of eternity' is nothing other than the *rahma* that streams forth from the divine Essence; and that this light, whose traces 'shimmer', as the Imam says, on the temples of *tawhid*, is reflected back to its source, through what he calls 'the attraction' of absolute unicity. This can be understood as the process by which divine love is consummated through the spiritual activity of *tawhid*, 'making one'. This attraction of oneness to the realisation of oneness is thus a kind of projection of the One to the multiple, and a reintegration of the multiple within the One. The outward manifestation of the 'hidden treasure' is magnetically 'charged', as it were, with the interiorizing power of merciful attraction. We might call this the cyclical motion of *tawhid*, a cycle beginning with *rahma* and ending with it: The following Qur'anic verse appears to allude to this: 'Truly, we belong to God, and truly unto Him we are returning' (Q 2:156).

Servants of *al-Rahman*

Let us now return to the *Du'a' Kumayl*. After being illumined by the lofty and subtle truth of all-embracing mercy, we are brought face to face with the gut-wrenching cry for mercy from a miserable sinner: 'O God, I find no forgiver of my sins, no concealer of my ugly acts, no transformer (*mubaddil*) of my ugly acts into beautiful ones, but You.' Here we have another allusion, this time to the promise of God given even to those guilty of idol-worship, murder, and adultery: if they repent, and have faith, and act virtuously, then not only will God forgive them, but, in the words of the Surat al-Furqan ('The Discernment', 25:70, noted earlier): 'God will transform (*yubaddil*) their ugly acts into beautiful ones.' The sinner addressing God in the supplication knows all too well that the magnetism of God's mercy cannot resist sincere repentance, and, as a truly repentant sinner, he is therefore emboldened to the point where he can confidently address God as follows:

> Can You see Yourself tormenting me with Your Fire, after I have professed Your unity? After the knowledge of You my heart has embraced, the remembrance of You my tongue has constantly mentioned, and the love of You to which my mind has clung? After the sincerity of my confession and my supplication, humble before Your lordship? Far be it from You!

> My Protector, how should he [the repentant sinner, i.e., himself] remain in the chastisement while he has hope for Your preceding clemency? Or how should the Fire cause him pain while he expects Your bounty and mercy?... Or how should he be convulsed among its levels while You know his sincerity?... Far be it from You! That is not what is expected of You, nor what is well known of Your grace.

What is 'well known' (*ma'ruf*) of God's grace is that His loving mercy 'encompasses all things,' for God has 'inscribed' on his very Self the principle of loving mercy (Q 6:12 and 6:54). The sinner knows this, and so does the sage. Imam 'Ali defines the true *faqih* in terms, precisely, of his knowledge of divine mercy. Let us remember that the word *faqih* means 'one who understands,' (cf. Q 9:122); only later did *fiqh* come to be identified almost exclusively with legal understanding. He says, 'The one who truly understands (*al-faqih*) among all those who understand is the one who never makes people despair of the mercy of God.' As we have just seen, one of the most remarkable things about the supplication of the sinner beseeching God through the *Du'a' Kumayl* is that he boldly tells God what he expects from Him: he refuses to despair of the mercy of God, however great be his sense of having sinned. The sinner is being taught, through Imam 'Ali and through the particular blessings associated with al-Khidr, what it means to say, as the Qur'an does in many places, that God forgives all sins, and that His mercy encompasses and thus prevails over all things, including His own wrath. The saying 'My Mercy takes precedence over My Wrath' is inscribed on the very Throne of God, according to the Prophet.

Let us note that al-Khidr is described in the Qur'an, in the Surat al-Kahf, as 'a servant from among Our servants, unto whom We had given *mercy* from Ourselves, and taught him knowledge from Our presence' (18:65). Mercy takes precedence over knowledge in this description of this mysterious personage whose knowledge surpassed even that of Moses. Similarly, the angels give priority to mercy over knowledge in their description of God's encompassing of all things: 'Those who bear the Throne, and all who are round about it, hymn the praises of their Lord, and believe in Him, and ask forgiveness for those who believe [saying]: "Our Lord, You encompass all things *in mercy and knowledge*"...' (Q 40:7).

It is as if one of the esoteric mysteries taught by al-Khidr in the Qur'an, and which is deeply sensed throughout the *Du'a' Kumayl*, is that authentic human knowledge is not only attuned to the reality of divine mercy, but that human knowledge itself is a grace granted by divine mercy. As the Qur'an tells us in the Surat al-Rahman: 'Al-Rahman taught the Qur'an, created man, taught him discernment' (55:1-4). Human knowledge emerges here as the result of the illuminating emanation of al-Rahman, as does the whole of creation, as we saw earlier. The implicit message here is that our knowledge of divine Reality will deepen in accordance with the attunement of our whole being to divine Mercy. 'He who shows no mercy will not have mercy shown to him (*man lam yarham lam yurham*),' said the Prophet; and Imam 'Ali echoes this in several sayings, as we saw earlier.

In Chapter 1, we noted that in the Imam's perspective, beauty of soul was essential to the integrity of intelligence. Here, we see how important the principle of loving mercy is for the proper functioning of the intelligence. One of the deeper implications of this teaching, at once ethical and intellectual, is this: if you are not merciful to others, you will not receive from God that particular grace which transforms your mental conceptions into heartfelt knowledge; your notional belief will not be transformed into deeper degrees of existential assimilation: heartfelt faith, unshakeable certainty, and liberating gnosis (*maʿrifa*)—such degrees of knowledge of God being referred to by Imam ʿAli as the *haqaʾiq al-iman* (spiritual realities of faith). It is only by virtue of these deeper degrees of faith, these spiritual modes of consciousness, that the heart is able to see God.

In the light of the Imam's teachings, we see that the true intellectual is one whose knowledge of reality, far from being abstract and cold, pulsates with love and mercy. From such a person, the light of knowledge will radiate as an almost tangible form of benevolent mercy, loving compassion. Such a person can be called an *ʿarif bi'Llah*, a term which has been translated appropriately as 'one who knows *through* God,' and not simply one who knows God. 'Know God through God,' says the Imam (*iʿrafu'Llah bi'Llah*), as noted earlier. One who knows God in this 'divine' way can be qualified as a 'lordly knower', *ʿalim rabbani* (cf. Q 3:79). This term is used by Imam ʿAli in another discourse to Kumayl, wherein he refers to three categories of people: the sage, the sincere seeker and the masses. Making one's knowledge 'lordly', *rabbani*, means absorbing into one's consciousness those qualities which most essentially define the Lord, *al-Rabb*, and these qualities are all summed up in the quality of *rahma*. As we saw in Chapter 1, the sages in this highest category, 'rejoice in their intimacy with the spirit of certainty; they make easy what the extravagant find harsh; they befriend that by which the ignorant are alienated. With their bodies they keep company with the world, while their spirits are tied to the transcendent realm.' These sages derive joy from the spirit of certainty (*ruh al-*

yaqin), because the object of their certainty—the divine Reality, *al-Haqiqa*—is pure beatitude.

In another discourse to Kumayl, Imam 'Ali mentions seven categories, and refers to the highest category of mankind as the 'servants of al-Rahman' (*'ibad al-Rahman*): they are outwardly modest and unimportant but inwardly steeped in an all-encompassing consciousness of God, from which the whole world benefits in an invisible way. They are described as follows:

> The seventh category is people whom God has praised, saying 'God's servants are those who tread lightly upon the earth; if the ignorant address them, they say "Peace!"' (Q 25:63)... They have taken the earth as bedding, its water as perfume, the Qur'an as garment, and prayer as robe. Their eyes weep, their clothing is dusty; and they have severed all ties with this world. If they leave, they are not missed, and if present they remain unknown. If they ask for a hand in marriage, they are refused, and if they speak they are not heeded. Yet it is because of them that God averts scourges, calamities, and trials from the world. It is because of them that God gives people water to drink, by sending rain from the sky, droplets from the clouds. They are the servants of God. Truly. Yes, truly (*haqqan, haqqan*) (Qutbuddin, *Treasury*, 65; translation modified).

In this passage we are given another dimension of meaning to the word *taqwa*. Earlier, this word was defined in terms of the whole range of pious attitudes, from fear of God to knowledge of God, its essence being awareness of God. But according to its etymology the root meaning is 'to protect'. The idea is that, through being always aware of God, one protects oneself against the consequences of disobeying God. Now, in the description given by Imam 'Ali here, he ascribes to these pious servants of al-Rahman a very different kind of protective function: despite their low status in the world, their permanent consciousness of God has veritably cosmic repercussions, for it is on account of their devotion to al-Rahman that He averts 'scourges, calamities and trials from the world.'

In this extraordinarily inspiring teaching, Imam 'Ali is telling us many things. One of them is this: he is teaching every person in society, from the poorest to the richest, that it is not their position in society that matters in the eyes of God. It is their *taqwa*, their consciousness of God, which is the decisive value from the divine point of view. For, as we saw earlier, in our discussion of Imam 'Ali's effort to rid Muslim society of the poisons of materialism and worldliness with which it had become infected, God defines nobility precisely in terms of *taqwa*: 'O mankind, the most noble of you, in the eyes of God, are those among you who are most conscious of God' (*atqakum*) (Q 49:13).

Through such servants of al-Rahman heavenly blessings flow to the whole world; it is on their account that God sustains His creation, because, as the Qur'an tells us, He only created creatures endowed with intelligence and free will 'in order that they might worship Me' (51:56). As the deepest purpose of creation is fulfilled by these sincere servants of God, He continues to provide sustenance for the whole world. We are reminded of the prophetic saying: 'The Last Hour will not come for as long as there is someone on earth saying "*Allah, Allah*".'

'If they leave, they are not missed, and if present they remain unknown.' The simple souls being described here belong to an 'invisible' community of saints: the contrast between political power and spiritual—or cosmic—authority is striking. One is reminded here of the first of the beatitudes preached by Jesus in the Sermon of the Mount: 'Blessed are the poor in spirit, for theirs is the kingdom of Heaven' (Matthew, 5:3). It is interesting to note the resemblance between the people described here by Imam 'Ali and those

Sufis who came to be known, some two centuries later, as 'the People of Blame' (al-Malamatiyya). Ibn 'Arabi described these saints as possessing the 'supreme degree' of sainthood, at the same time as being totally inconspicuous (Chittick, pp. 374–375).

There are numerous sayings of the Prophet in which individuals of low social standing are described as being not just elevated in the eyes of God, but also instrumental in maintaining God's sustenance for all creatures, and averting calamities from the world. They are often referred to as the *abdal*, 'substitutes', forty in number, according to several of these *hadiths*; when one of them dies, another takes his place. This idea was elaborated in later Sufi doctrine, with great detail and precision, by Ibn 'Arabi, according to whom the head of this hierarchy is the spiritual 'Pole' (al-qutb) of the age; that is, the person who unites within himself (or herself: for the Pole can be a woman, according to Ibn 'Arabi) Heaven and earth, Spirit and matter, and who is described by Ibn 'Arabi as 'the place of God's gaze' (Chodkiewicz, *Seal*, p. 58).

This takes us back to the timeless mystery of Imam 'Ali, for he was both the Pole of his age and 'the place of God's gaze'. Hence the Prophet could say, in what is perhaps his most direct allusion to the spiritual reality—the timeless mystery— of the Imam: 'Looking at the face of 'Ali is an act of worship.'

It is to this that we will now turn briefly.

Contemplating the 'Face' of the Imam

In his famous 'Sermon of Evidence' (*Khutbat al-bayan*), the Imam helps us to understand how a vision of his face can be described as an act of worship:

> I am the Sign of the All-Powerful. I am the gnosis of the mysteries. I am the Threshold of Thresholds. I am the companion of the radiance of the divine Majesty. I am

the First and the Last, the Manifest and the Hidden. I am
the Face of God. I am the mirror of God... I am he who
is in possession of the secret of God's Messenger.

Let us highlight three important points here:

1. Imam 'Ali describes himself as 'the Face of God' (*wajh
   Allah*).

2. He refers to himself as the 'mirror' (*mir'at*) of God.

3. He says that he knows the 'secret', or 'mystery' (*sirr*) of
   the Prophet.

Taking the first two points together: once we understand
that Imam 'Ali is a mirror of God, it is easy to see how he
can refer to himself as the Face of God: the face that we see
in the mirror is not that of the individual, 'Ali b. Abi Talib,
but the Face of God. The mirror, indeed, becomes invisible,
when we are really focusing upon that which is reflected in it.
This 'invisibility' of the mirror can be taken as the symbol of
the Imam's total self-effacement, his *fana' fi'Llah*, 'extinction
in God'. All the Names and Qualities of God can be seen
reflected in the mirror of the perfectly effaced saint. Hence,
the mirror can say, in an allusion to that which is reflected
in it, that 'it is' the First and the Last, together with all the
divine Names and Qualities: 'it is' each of these Names, only
as the locus of manifestation (*mazhar*) whereupon the Names
and Qualities are manifested, and not as these Names and
Qualities are in their unique Essence, eternally transcending
all manifestation. Hence, it is not surprising that nowhere—
not even in the most radical *ghuluww* literature—do we find
the Imam saying, 'I am the Essence of God.'

In the Sufi tradition the Prophet is described as a mirror
reflecting the Divine Nature. For example, the sixteenth
century Turkish poet, Khaqani, sings to the Prophet:

God made you the mirror of the Essence,

A looking-glass for the unique Essence.
(cited by Schimmel, *Muhammad*, 131)

Ibn 'Arabi helps us to appreciate the relationship between the prophetic mirror and our own spiritual quest: looking at the Prophetic reality, with the eye of the heart, means contemplating God in the most perfect manner possible.

> The manifestation of God in the mirror of the Prophet is the most perfect, the most accurate, and the most beautiful; when you perceive Him in the mirror of the Prophet you perceive a perfection that you cannot perceive when contemplating Him in your own mirror.... Therefore, do not try to contemplate God anywhere but in the mirror of the Prophet (Ibn 'Arabi, *Futuhat* (1329/1911 ed.), 3:251; see for discussion, Addas, 'Muhammadian House').

If we remember that the Prophet described 'Ali as being 'like my very soul' (*ka-nafsi*), we might not be wrong in speculating that when the Prophet said that looking at 'Ali is an act of worship, he was hinting at his own mystery as well as that of the Imam. The implication could well be that looking at himself was an even greater act of worship than looking at 'Ali. Out of modesty, however, and in the tradition of Arabic *balagha* (rhetoric), the veiled reference to his own spiritual reality is made even more mysterious by alluding to the presence of this reality in another person: the companion, the brother, the friend, the lover, who most faithfully reflects his own reality.

The relationship between seeing the Prophet and contemplating God is, however, explicitly found in such statements as the following: 'He who sees me, has seen the Truth' (*al-Haqq*). The exoteric interpretation of this saying, which is found both in authoritative Sunni collections (see for example, Bukhari, *Sahih*, 8:72) as well as in Shi'i sources, is that one who sees the Prophet in a dream has indeed seen his true form. The esoteric interpretation is self-evident, and indeed fits the literal wording more exactly. The following couplets in Rumi's *Mathnawi* reinforce this interpretation. They come in the context of a playful dialogue between Rumi and Shams, where the secret of the Friend (*Yar*, the Persian equivalent of *Wali*) is being teased out:

> It is better that the secret of the Friend should be disguised:
> do thou hearken (to it as implied) in the contents of the tale.
> It is better that the lovers' secret
> should be told in the talk of others.
> (*Mathnawi*, 1:134–135)

The last line could be rendered thus: 'it is sweeter that the mystery of the lovers be conveyed through speaking about others' (*hadith-e digaran*). It is as if Rumi is saying: let me allude to the mystery of my own sainthood by describing other saints—which is precisely what he does, not only in relation to Shams but also in relation to Husam al-Din and others. Rumi proclaims: 'Sweet is the oneness of the Friend with His friends' (*ittihad-i yar ba yaran*; *Mathnawi*, 1:682). So, to describe one of the friends of God, the saints, is to describe them all; by the same token, it is to allude to the Friend, *al-Wali*, God himself. For:

> Inasmuch as God comes not into sight, these prophets are the vicars (*nayeb*) of God.
> Nay, I have said wrongly; for if you suppose that the vicar and He who is represented by the vicar are two, it [such a thought] is bad, not good.
> Nay; they are two so long as you are a worshipper of form (*surat*), they have become one to him who has escaped from form.
> (*Mathnawi*, 1:674–675)

To escape from the worship of 'form' is tantamount to seeing the One in the mirror of all forms. 'Wherever you turn, there is the Face of God' (Q 2:115). When we look at 'Ali, we see the *mazhar al-'aja'ib* (as he is called in the famous *Nad-i 'Ali* formula): the place, the face, the mirror wherein are reflected 'marvels'. We see the manifestation (*zuhur*) of the marvellous Names and Qualities of the Face of God, God as *al-Zahir*, 'The Outwardly Apparent'. 'The believer is the mirror of the believer,' said the Prophet. We could also translate this as 'The believer is the mirror of the One who gives security through faith,' since *al-Mu'min* is one of the Names of God. When we look in the mirror of God, the mirror itself is invisible, we see only what is reflected in it, the Face. The manifestation of God is distinct from the Essence of God, even though the manifestation has no reality apart from That of which it is a manifestation. The Essence remains eternally invisible, ineffable, transcending all things, including Its own manifestation.

In this prophetic teaching, an infinite play of reflections becomes visible to the eye of the spiritual imagination. The human *mu'min* mirrors both the divine *Mu'min* and the human *mu'min*; mirroring them both, to both the human *mu'min*, and the divine, *al-Mu'min*, simultaneously, along vertical and horizontal axes, in a never-ending play of reflections upon reflections, *ad infinitum*. According to the Prophet, 'God is veiled by seventy thousand veils of light and darkness; were they to be removed, the glory of His Face would burn up all that He looked upon.' So, all we can see of the divine Light is what comes through veils, mirrors, symbols, and icons, one of the greatest of which is the face of a saint: the divine reality realised in the heart of the saint is reflected by the spiritual light which illumines the face of the saint, whence the saying *munawwar*, 'lit up', in describing the radiance one feels almost tangibly flowing from the face of a saint.

When Imam 'Ali tells us that God can be seen by the

heart through the *haqa'iq al-iman* (the spiritual realities of faith), the implication is that what he sees is identical to the quintessence of what he is: the theophany constituted by the Face of God can only be seen by the theophany constituted by the human heart. 'My Heaven cannot contain Me, My earth cannot contain Me, but the heart of my believing slave can contain Me,' according to a *hadith qudsi*. When Imam 'Ali sees the theophany, the Face of God 'everywhere', he sees by virtue of the same theophany immanent within his own heart; thus what is seen is identical with that which sees, the subject and the object of the vision are one and the same. When Imam 'Ali sees God, he sees what he truly is, in the inmost depths of his being: the inward theophany and the outward theophany are at one. When we look at the life, the teachings and the holiness of Imam 'Ali, we see not what we are, but what we can be: a true human being, made in the image of God. Contemplating the face of 'Ali's perfect sanctity reveals something of what is hidden in the depths of our own humanity.

> We shall show them Our signs on the horizons and in their own souls, until it becomes clear to them that He is the Real. Is it not enough that your Lord is the Witness of all things? (Surat Fussilat, 41:53)

Appendix
'Ali in the Sayings of the Holy Prophet

The following sayings of the Holy Prophet, drawn from highly authoritative Sunni sources, paint a kind of prophetic portrait, or *hilya*, of Imam 'Ali. Several of these sayings have been mentioned in the text, but putting them together in this way as a list might help us to see the Imam as the Holy Prophet saw him. Reflecting upon this prophetic portrait can also help to evoke Imam 'Ali's 'stellar' radiance in the constellation of Islamic spirituality.

⋄ 'For whomever I am the master (*mawla*), 'Ali is his master.'

⋄ 'I am the city of knowledge and 'Ali is its gate; so whoever desires knowledge, let him enter the gate.'

⋄ 'Truly, 'Ali is from me and I am from him, and he is the *wali* [synonym of *mawla*] of every believer after me.'

⋄ 'Ali is with the Quran and the Quran is with 'Ali. They will not separate from each other until they return to me at the pool [of Paradise].'

⋄ 'Three things were revealed to me regarding 'Ali: he is the leader of the Muslims, the guide of the pious and chief of the radiantly devout.

⋄ 'Looking at the face of 'Ali is an act of worship.'

⋄ 'May God have mercy on 'Ali. O God, make the truth revolve around 'Ali wherever he turns.'

⋄ 'O 'Ali, you are a leader (*sayyid*) in the world and the Hereafter. Your beloved is my beloved, and my beloved is the beloved of God; your enemy is my enemy, and my enemy is the enemy of God. Woe be to those who hate you after me [after I have passed away].'

⋄ 'Whoever desires to live my life and to die my death and to take his rest in the eternal Garden my Lord has promised me, let him orient himself towards 'Ali, for truly he will never cause you to depart from right guidance, nor cause you to enter into error.'

⋄ The Holy Prophet said that 'Ali was 'like my own soul' (*ka-nafsi*).

⋄ He said to 'Ali, 'You are from me and I am from you'.

⋄ '... whoever obeys 'Ali obeys me, and whoever disobeys him disobeys me.'

⋄ 'You will clarify for my community that over which they will differ after me.'

⋄ 'There is one amongst you who will fight for the interpretation of the Quran as I have fought for its revelation... it is he who is mending my sandal.' According to this report, Muhammad had given 'Ali his sandal to mend.

⋄ 'O 'Ali, there is in you something akin to Jesus, on whom be peace and blessings. The Jews hated him to such an extent that they slandered his mother; and the Christians loved him to such an extent that they ascribed to him a rank he did not possess.'

⋄ 'O 'Ali, whoever separates himself from me separates himself from God, and whoever separates himself from you, O 'Ali, separates himself from me.'

⋄ 'Whoever curses 'Ali curses me, and whoever curses me curses God.'

⋄ The Holy Prophet was reported to have asked his wife Aisha, 'Call unto me the leader (*sayyid*) of the Arabs.' She asked, 'O Prophet of God, are you not the leader of the Arabs?' He said, 'I am the leader of the children of Adam, and 'Ali is the leader of the Arabs.'

⋄ 'The first of you to enter the [paradisal] pool is the first of you who entered Islam, 'Ali.'

⋄ "Ali is from me and I am from him, and nobody can fulfil my duty but myself and 'Ali.'

⋄ Ali himself relates that the Holy Prophet had said to him that none but a believer will love him [Ali], and none but a hypocrite will hate him.

⋄ It is reported that when the Holy Prophet was about to depart for an expedition to Tabuk, he left 'Ali as his deputy in Medina. 'Ali was sad not to be joining him. The Holy Prophet said, 'Are you not happy that you should have in relation to me the rank of Aaron in relation to Moses, except that there is no prophet after me?'

⋄ It is reported that the Holy Prophet prayed to God to bring 'the most beloved of Your creatures' to partake with him in a meal of fowl. Others came but only when 'Ali came did the Holy Prophet ask him to join him and partake of the meal.

⋄ Among the several verses of the Quran which were apparently commented upon by the Holy Prophet with reference to Imam 'Ali is 13:7: 'Verily you are a warner, and for every people there is a guide.' The Holy Prophet is reported to have said, 'I am the warner... you are the guide, O 'Ali. After me, the rightly-guided shall be guided by you.'

⋄ Quran commentators relate verse 55 of Chapter 5 ('The Table Spread'), 'Verily your *wali* is only God and His Messenger and those who believe, establish the prayer and give alms while bowing in prayer,' to an incident when Imam 'Ali, whilst bowing in prayer, held out his ring for a beggar who had asked for alms. The Holy Prophet is reported to have recited this verse when told of the incident, and added the words already cited from the Ghadir hadith: 'For whomever I am the *mawla*, 'Ali is his *mawla*.'

⋄ Quran commentators report that when the Holy Prophet was asked about the identity of 'the best of creatures (*khayr al-bariyya*)', mentioned in Surat al-Bayyina (98:7), he replied: ''Ali and his Shi'a ('partisans').'

See for further discussion, Shah-Kazemi, *Justice and Remembrance*, pp. 18–22.

Bibliography

Addas, Claude. 'The Muhammadian House: Ibn 'Arabi's Concept of *ahl al-bayt*', in *Journal of the Muhyiddin Ibn 'Arabi Society*, vol. 50, 2011, 77–95.

——*Quest for Red Sulphur: The Life of Ibn 'Arabi*, tr. P. Kingsley. Cambridge, 1993.

'Ali b. Abi Talib. *Diwan*, ed. 'Abd al-Rahman al-Mustawi. Beirut and London, 2005.

——*Du'a' Kumayl*, tr. W.C. Chittick in *Supplications: Amir al-Mu'minin*. London, 1995.

——*Ghurar al-Hikam wa Durar al-Kalim*. Trans. as *Exalted Aphorisms and Pearls of Speech*, by Tahir Ridha Jaffer. Qom, 2012.

——*Nahj al-balagha*. Compiled by al-Sharif al-Radi. ed. 'Azizullah al-'Utaridi. Tehran, 1993;

Persian trans. Ja'far Shahidi. Tehran, 1378 Sh./1999;

English trans. Askari Jafery. Bombay, 1978;

English trans. Yasin T. al-Jibouri. 3 vols. Bloomington, 2013.

Amir-Moezzi, Mohammad 'Ali. *The Divine Guide in Early Shi'ism: The Sources of Esotericism in Islam*, tr. David Streight. New York, 1994.

——*The Spirituality of Shi'i Islam*, tr. Hafiz Karmali. London, 2011.

Amuli, Sayyid Haydar. *Jami' al-asrar*. Ed. H. Corbin and O. Yahya, in *La philosophie shi'ite*. Tehran-Paris. 1969.

'Attar, Farid al-Din. *Mantiq al-tayr*. Tehran, 1377 Sh./1998.

——*The Conference of the Birds*, tr. A. Darbandi & D. Davis. London, 1984.

Ayoub, Mahmoud M. *The Crisis of Muslim History: Religion and Politics in Early Islam*. Oxford, 2005.

al-Bukhari, Muhammad b. Isma'il. *Sahih al-Bukhari*. Beirut, Dar al-fikr, n.d.

Chirri, Mohammad Jawad. *The Brother of the Prophet Muhammad: The Imam 'Ali*. 2 vols. Detroit, 1982.

Chodkiewicz, Michel. *An Ocean Without Shore: Ibn 'Arabi, the Book and the Law*, tr. David Streight. New York, 1993.

——*Seal of the Saints: Prophethood and Sainthood in the Doctrine of Ibn 'Arabi*, tr. Liadain Sherrard. Cambridge, 1993.

Corbin, Henry. *Creative Imagination in the Sufism of Ibn 'Arabi*, tr. R. Mannheim. New Jersey, 1969.

——*En Islam iranien: Aspects spirituels et philosophiques*. 4 vols. Paris, 1971–1972.

——*Face de Dieu, Face de l'homme: Herméneutique et soufisme*. Paris, 2008.

——*History of Islamic Philosophy*, tr. Philip Sherrard. London, 1993.

Crow, Douglas Karim. 'Social and Economic Policies of Imam 'Ali: Insights for Intra-Muslim Accommodation'. (Forthcoming, in the online edition of *Encyclopaedia Islamica*, art. "Ali'.)

Daftary, Farhad, Amyn B. Sajoo and Shainool Jiwa (ed.). *The Shi'i World: Pathways in Tradition and Modernity*. London, 2015.

Daftary, Farhad and Gurdofarid Miskinzoda (ed.). *The Study of Shi'i Islam: History, Theology and Law*. London, 2014.

Dakake, Maria Massi. *The Charismatic Community: Shi'ite Identity in Early Islam*. Albany, New York, 2007.

Dashti, Mohammad (ed.). *Ma'arif-i Nahj al-balagha dar shi'r-i Farsi* ('Spiritual Wisdom of the *Nahj al-balagha* in the Poetry of the Poets'). Qom, 1996.

Eck, Diana L. *Darsan: Seeing the Divine Image in India*. Delhi, 2007.

Elmore, Gerald. *Islamic Sainthood in the Fullness of Time: Ibn al-'Arabi's Book of the Fabulous Gryphon*. Leiden, 1999.

al-Ghazali, Abu Hamid. *Kimiya-yi sa'adat* ('The Alchemy of Happiness'). Tehran, 1992.

——*Disciplining the Soul and Breaking the Two Desires: Books XXII and XXIII of the Revival of the Religious Sciences*. Tr. T. J. Winter. Cambridge, 1995.

Ghazi b. Muhammad, Ibrahim Kalin & Mohammad Hashim Kamali (eds). *War and Peace in Islam: The Uses and Abuses of Jihad.* Cambridge, 2013.

Guillaume, Alfred. *The Life of Muhammad: A Translation of Ibn Ishaq's Sirat Rasul Allah.* London, 1955.

Hafiz, Shams al-Din Muhammad, *Diwan.* Ed. A. A. Shirazi. Tehran, 1376 Sh./1997.

Hasan, Masudul. *Hadrat 'Ali Murtada.* New Delhi, 1998.

Hodgson, Marshall G. S. *The Venture of Islam: Conscience and History in a World Civilization.* 3 vols. Chicago & London, 1974.

Ibn 'Abd al-Barr, Yusuf. *Al-Isti'ab fi ma'rifat al-ashab* (ed.) 'Ali Muhammad al-Bajawi. Beirut, 1412/1992, 4 vols.

Ibn Abi'l-Hadid, 'Izz al-Din. *Sharh Nahj al-balagha*, ed. Muhammad Abu al-Fadl Ibrahim. 20 vols. Beirut, 1965–1967.

Ibn Abi Shayba, Abu Bakr. *al-Musannaf.* Riyadh, 2004.

Ibn al-'Arabi. *al-Futuhat al-Makkiyya.* Cairo, 1269/1853.

——*al-Futuhat al-Makkiyya.* Cairo, 1329/1911.

——*The Ringstones of Wisdom (Fusus al-hikam)*, tr. Caner Dagli. Chicago, 2004.

Ibn Mardawayh, Abu Bakr Ahmad. *Manaqib 'Ali b. Abi Talib.* Qom, 1382 Sh./2003.

Ibn Sa'd, Abu 'Abd Allah Muhammad. *al-Tabaqat al-kubra*, ed. Ihsan Abbas. Beirut, 1968.

Ibn Shahrashub, Abu Ja'far Muhammad. *Manaqib Al Abi Talib.* Qom, 1421/2000.

Ja'farian, Rasul. *History of the Caliphs: From the Death of the Messenger to the Decline of the Umayyad Dynasty, 11–132 AH*, tr. 'Ali Ebrahimi. Qom, 2003.

——*Tarikh-i tashayyu' dar Iran.* Qom, 1375Sh./1996.

——*Tarikh wa sirah-i siyasi-yi amir al-mu'minin 'Ali b. Abi Talib.* Qom, 1380 Sh./2001.

Jafri, S. Husain M. *Origins and Early Development of Shi'a Islam.* London and New York, 1979.

Jawadi-Amuli, 'Abd Allah. *Life of Gnosis: A Mystical Study of Imam 'Ali's Life.* New Jersey, 2014.

159

Jibouri, Yasin T. *Path of Eloquence: Nahj al-Balagha*. 3 vols. Blooming-ton, 2013.

Jordac, George. *The Voice of Human Justice*. Qom, 2012.

al-Kashani, 'Abd al-Razzaq. *Tafsir Ibn 'Arabi* [erroneously ascribed to Ibn 'Arabi]. Cairo, n.d.

Lalljee, Yousuf. *'Ali the Magnificent*. New York, 1981.

Lewisohn, Leonard. "'Ali Ibn Abi Talib's Ethics of Mercy in the Mirror of Persian Sufism'. In M. Ali Lakhani (ed.), *The Sacred Foundations of Justice in Islam: The Teachings of Ali ibn Abi Talib*. Bloomington, 2006, pp. 109–145.

Lings, Martin. *Muhammad: His Life Based on the Earliest Sources*. Cambridge, 1991.

Madelung, Wilferd. *The Succession to Muhammad: A Study of the Early Caliphate*. Cambridge, 1997.

Massignon, Louis. 'Élie et son role transhistorique, Khadiriyya, en Islam', in Gustave Bardy (ed.) *Élie le prophète*, vol. 2, *Au Carmel dans le Judaïsme et l'Islam*. Bruges, 1956, 269–289.

——*The Passion of al-Hallaj: Mystic and Martyr of Islam*, tr. Herbert Mason. New Jersey, 1982.

al-Mufid, Shaykh (Muhammad b. Muhammad b. Nu'man al-Baghdadi). *Kitab al-irshad* (The Book of Guidance), tr. I. K. A. Howard. London, 1981.

——*The Battle of the Camel*, tr. I. K. A. Howard & J. A. Hamidi. London, 2014.

Mutahhari, Murtada. *Glimpses of the Nahj al-balagha*. Tehran, 1997.

al-Nasa'i, Ahmad b. Shu'ayb, *The Special Characteristics of the Leader of the Faithful: 'Ali b. Abi Talib*, tr. Michael Mumisa. Birmingham, 2014.

Nasr, Seyyed Hossein. *Sufi Essays*. London, 1972.

Pakatchi, Ahmad. *Mawlid Amir al-mu'minin: Nusus mustakhraja min al-turath al-islami*. Qom, 1382 Sh./2003.

Perry, Whitall. *Treasury of Traditional Wisdom*. London, 1971.

al-Qummi, Abu Hasan 'Ali b. Ibrahim. *Tafsir al-Qummi*. Beirut, 1991.

Qutbuddin, Tahera. *A Treasury of Virtues: Sayings, Sermons, and Teachings of 'Ali, with the One Hundred Proverbs Attributed to al-Jahiz*. New York, 2013.

Razi, Fakhr al-Din. *Al-Tafsir al-kabir*. Beirut, 2001.

Rubin, Uri. 'Pre-Existence and Light—Aspects of the Concept of *Nur Muhammad*', in *Israel Oriental Studies* 5 (1975), 62–119.

Rumi, Jalal al-Din. *Discourses (Fihi ma fihi)*, tr. A. J. Arberry. London, 1961.

——*Kulliyyat-i Shams (Diwan-i Kabir)*, ed. Badi' al-Zaman Furuzanfar. 10 vols. Tehran, 1378 Sh./1999.

——*The Mathnawi of Jalalu'ddin Rumi*, tr. R. A. Nicholson. 3 vols. London, 1926.

Al-Saffar al-Qummi, Abu Ja'far Muhammad. *Basa'ir al-darajat*. Tehran, 1384/1995.

Sallabi, 'Ali Muhammad. *Asma al-matalib fi sira amir al-mu'minin 'Ali bin Abi Talib*. 2 vols. Riyadh, 2004.

Schaya, Leo. 'The Mission of Elias', in *Studies in Comparative Religion*, vol. 14, nos. 3-4, 1980, 159-167.

Schimmel, Annemarie. *And Muhammad is His Messenger—The Veneration of the Prophet in Islamic Piety*. Chapel Hill and London, 1985.

Scholem, Gershom. *Origins of the Kabbalah*. Berlin, 1962.

Schuon, Frithjof. *Understanding Islam*, tr. M. Perry, J-P Lafouge. Bloomington, 2011.

Al-Shafi'i, Muhammad b. Idris. *Diwan*, ed. Ihsan 'Abbas. Beirut, 1996.

Shah-Kazemi, Reza. 'Blessing the Prophet: Purifying the Heart', in *Sacred Web: A Journal of Tradition and Modernity*, no. 33, 2014, 139-166.

——*Justice and Remembrance: Introducing the Spirituality of Imam 'Ali*. London, 2006.

——*Paths to Transcendence: According to Shankara, Ibn 'Arabi and Meister Eckhart*. Bloomington, 2006.

——*Spiritual Quest: Reflections on Qur'anic Prayer according to the Teachings of Imam 'Ali*. London, 2011.

——*The Spirit of Tolerance in Islam*. London, 2012.

Shah-Kazemi, Reza et al. ''Ali' in *Encyclopaedia Islamica*, editors-in-chief W. Madelung, F. Daftary, London, 2011, vol. 3, 477–583.

Sobhani, Ja'far. *Doctrines of Shi'i Islam: A Compendium of Imami Beliefs and Practices*, tr. R. Shah-Kazemi. London, 2001.

al-Suyuti, Jalal al-Din. *Al-Durr al-manthur fi'l-tafsir bi'l-ma'thur*. Beirut, 1314/1896.

——*History of the Caliphs*, tr. H. S. Jarrett. Amsterdam, 1970.

al-Tabari, Abu Ja'far Muhammad. *Jami' al-bayan*. Beirut, 2001.

——*The History of al-Tabari*. vol. 6: *Muhammad at Mecca*, tr. W. Montgomery Watt and M. V. McDonald. New York, 1988.

——*The History of al-Tabari*. vol. 15, *The Crisis of the Early Caliphate—The Reign of Uthman, A.D. 644–656/A.H. 24–35*, tr. R. Stephen Humphreys. New York, 1990.

——*The History of al-Tabari*. vol. 16, *The Community Divided—The Caliphate of 'Ali, A.D. 656–657/ A.H. 35–36*, tr. Adrian Brockett. New York, 1997.

——*The History of al-Tabari*. vol. 17, *The First Civil War—From the Battle of Siffin to the Death of 'Ali, A.D. 656–661/ A.H. 36–40*, tr. G.R. Hawting. New York, 1996.

Tabataba'i, Sayyid Muhammad Husayn. *Kernel of the Kernel: Concerning the Wayfaring and Spiritual Journeying of the People of the Intellect*, tr. Mohammad H. Faghfoory. Albany, New York, 2003.

Tirmazi, Syed Ahmad Irshad. *'Ali: The Manifesting Imam*. Lahore, 2007.

Upton, Charles. *The Virtues of the Prophet*. San Rafael, 2006.

Walshe. M.O'C. *Meister Eckhart: Sermons & Treatises*. Dorset, 1971.

Williams, Rowan. *Ponder These Things: Praying with Icons of the Virgin*. Norwich, 2002.

Yusufiyan, Hasan and Sharifi, Ahmad. *'Imam 'Ali wa mukhalifan'* ('Imam 'Ali and his Opponents'), in A. A. Rashad (ed.), *Danish-namah-i Imam 'Ali*, vol. 6, pp. 238–246. Tehran, 2001.

General Index